Telecommunications Law and Policy
Second Edition

2007 Supplement

Stuart M. Benjamin

Howard A. Shelanski

Philip J. Weiser

Carolina Academic Press
Durham, North Carolina

ISBN: 978-1-59460- 472 - 0

Carolina Academic Press
700 Kent Street
Durham, North Carolina 27701
Telephone (919) 489-7486
Fax (919) 493-5668
E-mail: cap@cap-press.com
www.cap-press.com

Table of Contents

Chapter 4: Structuring and Assigning Licenses

Insert Note 4 on p. 136:

4.   **Déjà vu All Over Again?** The day of comparative hearings and licenses issued without an auction appeared to be past, but two recent proposals suggested that parties have not given up hope that the FCC might be willing to dispense with the auction requirement. In 2006, CyrenCall filed a petition promising to build a next generation wireless broadband network for public safety agencies if the FCC issues a 30 MHz license in the 700 MHz band to a Public Broadband Trust (which, in turn, could contract with CyrenCall to build the network). This petition came on the heels of one by the firm M2Z, which promises to build a free wireless broadband network (including access for public safety) if the FCC issues it a 20 MHz license. The FCC rejected the first petition on the ground that Congress had already specified the need to auction the licenses in the 700 MHz band by statute. As to the M2Z proposal, the FCC had yet to rule on it as of June 2007, but if it does accept the concept of awarding a license without an auction, it may well use a comparative hearings procedure to ensure that M2Z, and not some other firm, is best positioned to deliver on the proposed plan.

Add after the notes on p. 186:

Some of the most significant licenses available for auction will emerge from the transition away from analog to digital TV (see Chapter 6). The frequencies being cleared in the 700 MHz band, which historically were used for UHF broadcasting (channels 52-69), will be auctioned at the end of 2007. Of course, the winners of the auction will have to wait until early 2009 (when the DTV transition is complete) to begin using the spectrum. Nonetheless, this auction has attracted significant interest both from existing players and new entrants, as it presents a unique opportunity to obtain licenses to "beachfront spectrum"—i.e., frequencies with very desirable propagation characteristics—and in greater amounts than are likely to become available for quite some time. Notably, the completion of the digital transition will not only give rise to the auctioning off of 60 MHz of prime spectrum, but also the delivery of 24 MHz of spectrum to public safety agencies. During the tragic events of September 11, 2001 and the aftermath of Hurricane Katrina, different public safety agencies (say, fire and police) could not communicate with one another, resulting in the loss of additional lives. These events underscore that facilitating interoperability and developing next generation services are essential goals for public safety and can be facilitated by this additional spectrum.

In evaluating the proper band plan for the 700 MHz band, the FCC has sought to spur the development of a next generation network to support greater functionality and interoperability in public safety communications. The excerpt below is the FCC's Ninth Notice of Proposed Rulemaking in a longstanding inquiry into how to structure public safety's use of new wireless spectrum.

Implementing a Nationwide, Broadband, Interoperable Public Safety Network in the 700 MHz Band
Ninth Notice of Proposed Rulemaking, 21 FCC Rcd. 14837 (2006)

I.   INTRODUCTION

1.   In the Commission's Eighth Notice of Proposed Rulemaking, the Commission sought comment on whether certain channels within the current 24 megahertz of public safety

spectrum in the 700 MHz band (764-776 MHz and 794-806 MHz) should be modified to accommodate broadband communications. . . .

2.   As also noted in the *Eighth NPRM*, the Commission previously announced principles for ensuring effective public safety use of the 700 MHz band, including standardization necessary to achieve nationwide interoperability, development of competitive equipment markets, and a degree of regional flexibility necessary to allow opportunities for tailored approaches to meeting the needs of regional communities.   The Commission also noted that Congress has recognized that the 700 MHz spectrum is "ideal" for providing first responders with interoperable communications channels, and established February 17, 2009 as the date by which this spectrum will be cleared of incumbent broadcasters.   Furthermore, the Commission found, in its Report to Congress submitted pursuant to the Intelligence Reform Act, that deployment of an integrated, nationwide, interoperable network capable of delivering broadband communications would offer the public safety community many benefits, including video surveillance, real-time text messaging and email, high resolution digital images and the ability to obtain location and status information of personnel and equipment in the field.   We thus are presented with an opportunity to put into place a regulatory framework that would ensure the availability of effective spectrum in the 700 MHz band for interoperable, public safety use.

4.   Our proposed plan is a departure from prior public safety allocations, and is designed to speed deployment, decrease costs of roll-out, promote nationwide interoperability and provide a source of funding for constructing a broadband public safety communications network. The proposal includes that the Commission (1) allocate 12 megahertz of the 700 MHz public safety spectrum from wideband to broadband use; (2) assign this spectrum nationwide to a single national public safety broadband licensee; (3) permit the national public safety broadband licensee also to operate on a secondary basis on all other public safety spectrum in the 700 MHz band; (4) permit the licensee to use its assigned spectrum to provide public safety entities with public safety broadband service on a fee for service basis; (5) permit the licensee to provide unconditionally preemptible access to its assigned spectrum to commercial service providers on a secondary basis; (6) facilitate the shared use of commercial mobile radio service (CMRS) infrastructure for the efficient provision of public safety broadband service; and (7) establish performance requirements for interoperability, build out, preemptibility of commercial access, and system robustness.

II.   BACKGROUND

5.   The current band plan for the public safety portion of the 700 MHz band provides narrowband (voice and low speed data) and wideband (image/high speed data and slow scan video) communications channels.   The allocation of the 700 MHz band between narrowband and wideband channels is depicted in Figure 1.   The four narrowband segments are 764-767 MHz, 773-776 MHz, 794-797 MHz, and 803-806 MHz.   [Noting, among other things, that "a large portion of the 700 MHz public safety spectrum, approximately 53 percent (12.5 megahertz), is designated for general use by local, regional and state users" and "[a] regional planning process was adopted to govern management of this public safety spectrum."]

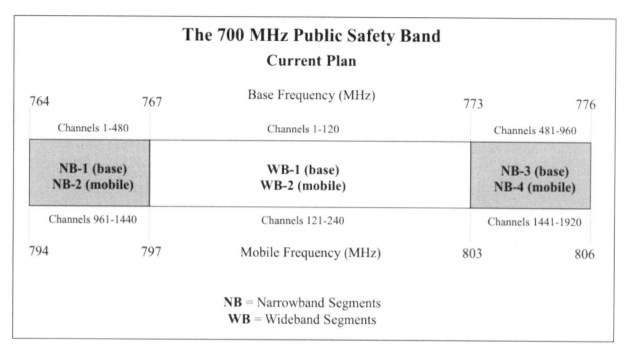

III. DISCUSSION

11.   We believe that the time may have come for a significant departure from the typical public safety allocation model the Commission has used in the past. In prior allocations for public safety, individual public safety jurisdictions have been able to apply for and utilize individual licenses. The Commission also has permitted public safety regional planning committees to develop plans for frequency coordination on a regional basis. While this system has had significant benefits for public safety users, in terms of permitting them to deploy voice and narrowband facilities suitable for their needs, the system also has resulted in uneven build-out across the country in different bands, balkanization of spectrum between large numbers of incompatible systems, and interoperability difficulties if not inabilities. In developing our proposal, we are guided by the following objectives for public safety communications in the twenty-first century.

A.   Objectives of Public Safety Model

12.   *Broadband.* Presently, there is no allocation in the 700 MHz public safety band for broadband communications. Broadband technologies hold the potential to provide public safety entities integrated access to voice and high-speed data capabilities, and thus may dramatically reduce the time it takes to access information during emergencies. We believe that we should maximize opportunities for broadband use of 700 MHz spectrum due to the many benefits of broadband communications, including video surveillance, real-time text messaging and email, high resolution digital images and the ability to obtain location and status information of personnel and equipment in the field. For example, police officers could exchange mug shots, fingerprints, photographic identification, and enforcement records; firefighters could have access to floor and building plans and real-time medical information; forensic experts could provide high resolution photographs of crime scenes and real-time video monitoring transmitted to incident command centers.

13.   *Nationwide Interoperability.* All emergency personnel involved in an incident

need to be able to communicate seamlessly. The availability of a nationwide, interoperable, broadband communications network for public safety substantially could enhance the ability of public safety entities to respond to emergency situations, whether due to severe weather events or criminal or terrorist activities, and likely would save lives and preserve property. Yet, only 2.6 megahertz is designated for nationwide interoperable communications in the 700 MHz public safety band. Furthermore, the radios used by federal, state and local first responders generally are not interoperable. Instead, the highly fragmented structure of public safety agencies, whether among different public safety agencies serving the same community (*i.e.*, local police, fire, emergency medical), neighboring communities or states, or among local, state, and federal levels, has resulted in many different and distinct communications infrastructures. As a consequence, public safety personnel often must carry multiple radios to coordinate their activities. Even when some interoperability is reached on a regional level, there still is a lack of nationwide interoperability.

18.   *Flexible Modern Architecture.* A public safety communications network employing modern IP-based wireless system architecture may have many advantages in terms of flexibility, cost and compatibility with the existing IP-based networks. An IP-based broadband wireless public safety system also readily could be integrated with legacy public safety and other wireless non-IP systems. IP-based architecture provides great flexibility in combining multiple services, *e.g.* voice, data and video, on a common infrastructure and into the same device.

B.   Proposal

19.   We propose that the 12 megahertz of spectrum at 767-773 MHz and 797-803 MHz, currently designated as wideband segments, be allocated for broadband use and that a single, national public safety broadband licensee be assigned this spectrum on a primary basis. The licensee also would be authorized to use all other public safety spectrum in the 700 MHz band on a secondary basis. Using this spectrum, the licensee would be authorized to provide public safety agencies voluntary access to broadband services, on a fee-for-service basis. The licensee also would be permitted to provide unconditionally preemptible access to this spectrum to commercial entities through leases or in the form of public/private partnerships. The national public safety broadband licensee may enter into arrangements with commercial service providers for accessing or sharing their communications systems infrastructure in order to create the nationwide, interoperable, broadband public safety communications network. We would leave significant discretion to the national licensee to carry out its responsibilities. We believe, however, that it would be necessary for the Commission to establish certain baseline performance requirements, including those for broadband, interoperability, build-out of national coverage, unconditional preemption of commercial use, and disaster restoration capability. We seek comment broadly on our proposed approach or any alternatives, as well as any potential impact on existing operations or planning activities by public safety in this spectrum.

1.   Single National Public Safety License

20.   A central theme of our proposal is the licensing of a single, national public safety entity for the provision of public safety broadband service in lieu of the traditional practice of licensing individual state and local jurisdictions. We believe that centralizing the licensee responsibilities into a single entity representative of the public safety community could best serve the objectives discussed above. A centralized, national network providing a wide range of communications services on a broadband backbone, using a flexible, modern architecture, could (1) enable nationwide interoperability; (2) reduce costs; (3) increase efficiency of spectrum usage; and (4) enhance network robustness.

5.   Secondary Operations in Public Safety Spectrum in the 700 MHz Band

38.   Under our proposal, the national public safety broadband licensee would be permitted to operate on a secondary basis on the remaining 12 megahertz of public safety spectrum in the 700 MHz band, *i.e.*, the narrowband channels. By secondary we mean that the national public safety licensee (1) may not interfere with primary use; (2) must immediately remedy any interference it causes to primary uses at its own expense (or shut down the interfering use); and (3) must accept any interference it receives from primary uses that are operating in accord with their licenses. One way to ensure that existing uses are not impacted may be through the employment of advanced technologies, such as cognitive radios.

39.   We believe that permitting the national licensee to use narrowband public safety spectrum in the 700 MHz band on a secondary basis significantly could increase the amount of spectrum available for broadband public safety use. Such secondary use also could provide a migration path for a gradual transition to the nationwide, interoperable, broadband public safety communications system from legacy narrowband systems. We anticipate that the national system can integrate voice and data capabilities into a single broadband communications network.

NOTES AND QUESTIONS

1.   **The Best Laid Plans . . .** The Commission's longstanding docket evaluating the proper treatment of the 24 MHz of wireless spectrum dedicated to public safety has allowed it to change course at the last minute. As the Order discusses, the original conception was that the spectrum would be used for narrowband and wideband communications. But the advent of broadband connectivity, which is increasingly becoming the *sine qua non* of modern communications, has upended the Commission's earlier plans. To facilitate the development of broadband networks for public safety agencies, the Commission proposed a radically new approach to public safety spectrum: the selection of a single national licensee.

2.   **Private Proposals to Enhance Public Safety Communications.** The political appeal of addressing the concerns related to a lack of interoperability and antiquated communications networks have led private firms to develop proposals to facilitate the development of a next generation network for public safety. As noted above, both CyrenCall and M2Z have suggested that spectrum be dedicated without an auction to support, among other things, public safety communications. In a variant of this approach, Frontline Wireless has suggested that a block of spectrum set to be auctioned (i.e., 10 MHz) be encumbered with a requirement to work with public safety and support the deployment of a next generation network for public safety. In practice, it seems likely that such a proposal would use the 10 MHz in conjunction with the 12 MHz held by the national public safety licensee.

3.   **Convergence in Public Safety Communications.** The culture of public safety communications has been, for its entire history, one of silo-based systems, with each individual local agency purchasing its own specialized equipment. The proposals for a national, broadband network, however, envision using "commercial off-the-shelf" equipment, the Internet Protocol standard, and a network that serves both public safety agencies and commercial users. This development, if implemented, would mark a radical public policy change. As some commentators suggest, it is also one that is long overdue. *See* Philip J. Weiser, Clearing the Air: Convergence and the Safety Enterprise (Aspen Institute 2006).

4.   **Public Safety's Use of Secondary Markets.** A second form of convergence noted by the above order is the suggested allowance of leasing spectrum dedicated to public safety agencies to commercial firms. This flexible use of spectrum would undermine the rigid

distinction between spectrum dedicated to public safety agencies and commercial providers. Is this step a wise one? How might it backfire?

Chapter 5:   Public Trustee Obligations

Insert the following immediately before note 4 on page 299:

The FCC's crackdown on offensive language hit a brick wall in the form of the Second Circuit's review of its ruling about Bono's comment at the Golden Globes and the claim that the word "fuck" constituted indecency.   The Second Circuit opinion and Judge Leval's dissent are excerpted below:

FOX TELEVISION STATIONS, INC. v. FCC
2007 WL 1599032 (2d Cir. June 4, 2007).

Opinion for the Court filed by Circuit Judge POOLER, in which Circuit Judge HALL concurs. Dissenting opinion filed by Circuit Judge LEVAL.

POOLER, Circuit Judge:

Fox Television Stations, Inc., along with its affiliates FBC Television Affiliates Association (collectively "Fox"), petition for review of the November 6, 2006, order of the Federal Communications Commission ("FCC") issuing notices of apparent liability against two Fox broadcasts for violating the FCC's indecency and profanity prohibitions. Fox, along with other broadcast networks and numerous amici, raise administrative, statutory, and constitutional challenges to the FCC's indecency regime. The FCC, also supported by several amici, dispute each of these challenges. We find that the FCC's new policy regarding "fleeting expletives" represents a significant departure from positions previously taken by the agency and relied on by the broadcast industry. We further find that the FCC has failed to articulate a reasoned basis for this change in policy. Accordingly, we hold that the FCC's new policy regarding "fleeting expletives" is arbitrary and capricious under the Administrative Procedure Act. The petition for review is therefore granted, the order of the FCC is vacated, and the matter is remanded to the Commission for further proceedings consistent with this opinion. Because we vacate the FCC's order on this ground, we do not reach the other challenges to the FCC's indecency regime raised by petitioners, intervenors, and amici.

BACKGROUND

The FCC's policing of "indecent" speech stems from 18 U.S.C. §1464, which provides that "[w]hoever utters any obscene, indecent, or profane language by means of radio communication shall be fined under this title or imprisoned not more than two years, or both." The FCC's authority to regulate the broadcast medium is expressly limited by Section 326 of the Communications Act, which prohibits the FCC from engaging in censorship. *See* 47 U.S.C. §326. In 1960, Congress authorized the FCC to impose forfeiture penalties for violations of Section 1464. The FCC first exercised its statutory authority to sanction indecent (but non-obscene) speech in 1975, when it found Pacifica Foundation's radio broadcast of comedian George Carlin's "Filthy Words" monologue indecent and subject to forfeiture. *See Citizen's Complaint Against Pacifica Found. Station WBAI(FM), N.Y, N.Y.,* 56 F.C.C.2d 94 (1975). True to its title, the "Filthy Words" monologue contained numerous expletives in the course of a 12-minute monologue broadcast on the radio at 2:00 in the afternoon. In ruling on this complaint, the FCC articulated the following description of "indecent" content:

> [T]he concept of 'indecent' is intimately connected with the exposure of children to language that describes, in terms patently offensive as measured by contemporary

community standards for the broadcast medium, sexual or excretory activities and organs, at times of the day when there is a reasonable risk that children may be in the audience. Obnoxious, gutter language describing these matters has the effect of debasing and brutalizing human beings by reducing them to their mere bodily functions, and we believe that such words are indecent within the meaning of the statute and have no place on radio when children are in the audience.

* * *

In its brief to the Supreme Court [in *Pacifica*], the FCC stressed that its ruling was a narrow one applying only to the specific facts of the Carlin monologue. *See* Br. of FCC at 41-49, *FCC v. Pacifica Found.*, No. 77-528 (U.S. Mar. 3, 1978), *available at* 1978 WL 206838. The Court took the Commission at its word and confined its review to the specific question of whether the Commission could find indecent the Carlin monologue as broadcast. *See FCC v. Pacifica Found.*, 438 U.S. 726, 732-35 (1978). . . . The Court therefore found that the FCC could, consistent with the First Amendment, regulate indecent material like the Carlin monologue. The Court then once again "emphasize[d] the narrowness of our holding . . . We simply hold that when the Commission finds that a pig has entered the parlor, the exercise of its regulatory power does not depend on proof that the pig is obscene." *Id.* at 750-51.

* * *

The FCC took the *Pacifica* Court's admonitions seriously in its subsequent decisions. [FN: At the time, the Commission interpreted *Pacifica* as involving a situation "about as likely to occur again as Halley's Comet." Br. of Amici Curiae Former FCC Officials at 6 (quoting FCC Chairman Charles D. Ferris, Speech to New England Broad. Assoc., Boston, Mass. (July 21, 1978)).] Shortly after the *Pacifica* ruling, the FCC stated the following in an opinion rejecting a challenge to a broadcaster's license renewal on the basis that the broadcaster had aired indecent programming:

> With regard to 'indecent' or 'profane' utterances, the First Amendment and the 'no censorship' provision of Section 326 of the Communications Act severely limit any role by the Commission and the courts in enforcing the proscription contained in Section 1464. The Supreme Court's decision in *FCC v. Pacifica Foundation*, 46 U.S.L.W. 5018 (1978), No. 77-528, decided July 3, 1978, affords this Commission no general prerogative to intervene in any case where words similar or identical to those in Pacifica are broadcast over a licensed radio or television station. *We intend strictly to observe the narrowness of the Pacifica holding.* In this regard, the Commission's opinion, as approved by the Court, relied in part on the repetitive occurrence of the 'indecent' words in question. The opinion of the Court specifically stated that it was not ruling that 'an occasional expletive . . . would justify any sanction . . . Further, Justice Powell's concurring opinion emphasized the fact that the language there in issue had been 'repeated over and over as a sort of verbal shock treatment.' He specifically distinguished 'the verbal shock treatment [in *Pacifica*]' from 'the isolated use of a potentially offensive word in the course of a radio broadcast.'

Application of WGBH Educ. Found., 69 F.C.C.2d 1250, at ¶10 (1978) (emphasis added) (ellipses in original; internal footnotes and citations omitted).

The FCC also specifically held that the single use of an expletive in a program that aired at

5:30pm "should not call for us to act under the holding of *Pacifica.*" *Id.* at ¶10 n. 6. A few years later, the Commission again rejected a challenge to a license renewal that complained the broadcaster had aired indecent programming in violation of Section 1464. The FCC acknowledged the complaint that the broadcaster on three separate occasions had aired programming during the morning hours containing language such as "motherfucker," "fuck," and "shit," but nevertheless concluded that "it is clear that the petitioner has failed to make a *prima facie* case that [the broadcaster] has violated 18 U.S.C. 1464 "since the language did not amount to "verbal shock treatment" and the complainant had failed to show this was more than "isolated use." *Application of Pacifica Found.,* 95 F.C.C.2d 750, at ¶¶16, 18 (1983).

It was not until 1987 that the FCC would find another broadcast "indecent" under Section 1464. *See Infinity Broad. Corp., et al.,* 3 F.C.C.R. 930 (1987) ("Infinity Order"). The Commission explained:

> In cases decided subsequent to the Supreme Court's ruling [in *Pacifica*], the Commission took a very limited approach to enforcing the prohibition against indecent broadcasts. Unstated, but widely assumed, and implemented for the most part through staff rulings, was the belief that only material that closely resembled the George Carlin monologue would satisfy the indecency test articulated by the FCC in 1975. Thus, no action was taken unless material involved the repeated use, for shock value, of words similar or identical to those satirized in the Carlin "Filthy Words" monologue . . . As a result, the Commission, since the time of its ruling in 1975, has taken no action against any broadcast licensee for violating the prohibition against indecent broadcasts.

Id. at ¶4 (internal footnotes omitted).

* * *

This restrained enforcement policy would continue. In 2001, pursuant to a settlement agreement by which the FCC agreed to clarify its indecency standards, the Commission issued a policy statement to "provide guidance to the broadcast industry regarding our case law interpreting 18 U.S.C. §1464 and our enforcement policies with respect to broadcast indecency." *Industry Guidance on the Commission's Case Law Interpreting 18 U.S.C. §1464,* 16 F.C.C.R. 7999, at ¶1 & ¶30 n. 23 (2001) ("Industry Guidance"). The FCC first noted that "indecent speech is protected by the First Amendment, and thus, the government must both identify a compelling interest for any regulation it may impose on indecent speech and choose the least restrictive means to further that interest." *Id.* at ¶3.

* * *

This restrained enforcement policy would soon change. During NBC's January 19, 2003, live broadcast of the Golden Globe Awards, musician Bono stated in his acceptance speech "this is really, really, fucking brilliant. Really, really, great." *Complaints Against Various Broadcast Licensees Regarding Their Airing of the "Golden Globe Awards" Program,* 19 F.C.C.R. 4975, at ¶3 n. 4 (2004) ("Golden Globes"). Individuals associated with the Parents Television Council filed complaints that the material was obscene and indecent under FCC regulations. *Id.* at ¶3. The FCC's Enforcement Bureau, however, denied the complaints on the basis that the expletive as used in context did not describe sexual or excretory organs or activities and that the utterance was fleeting and isolated. *See Complaints Against Various Broadcast Licensees Regarding Their Airing of the "Golden Globe Awards" Program,* 18 F.C.C.R. 19859, at ¶¶5-6 (Enforcement

Bureau 2003) ("Golden Globes (Bureau Decision)"). The Bureau accordingly found that the speech "does not fall within the scope of the Commission's indecency prohibition," and reaffirmed FCC policy that "fleeting and isolated remarks of this nature do not warrant Commission action ." *Id.* at ¶6.

Five months later, the full Commission reversed the Bureau's decision. First, the FCC held that any use of any variant of "the F-Word" inherently has sexual connotation and therefore falls within the scope of the indecency definition. *Golden Globes,* at ¶8. The FCC then held that "the 'F-Word' is one of the most vulgar, graphic, and explicit descriptions of sexual activity in the English language" and therefore the use of that word was patently offensive under contemporary community standards. *Id.* at ¶9. The Commission found the fleeting and isolated use of the word irrelevant and overruled all prior decisions in which fleeting use of an expletive was held not indecent. *Id.* at ¶12 ("While prior Commission and staff action have indicated that isolated or fleeting broadcasts of the 'F-Word' such as that here are not indecent or would not be acted upon, consistent with our decision today we conclude that any such interpretation is no longer good law.").

The FCC then held that the material in question was also "profane" under Section 1464. *Id.* at ¶13. The Commission acknowledged that prior decisions interpreting "profane" had defined that term as blasphemy, but found that nothing in its prior decisions limited the definition of profane in such a manner. *Id.* at ¶14. The Commission, however, declined to impose a forfeiture because "existing precedent would have permitted this broadcast" and therefore NBC and its affiliates "necessarily did not have the requisite notice to justify a penalty." *Id.* at ¶15. The Commission emphasized, though, that licensees were now on notice that any broadcast of the "F-Word" could subject them to monetary penalties and suggested that implementing delay technology would ensure future compliance with its policy. *Id.* at ¶17.

NBC, along with several other parties including Fox, filed petitions for reconsideration of the *Golden Globes* order, raising statutory and constitutional challenges to the new policy. NBC, Fox, and Viacom Inc. also filed a joint petition to stay the effect of the *Golden Globes* order. These petitions have been pending for more than two years without any action by the FCC. Nevertheless, the FCC has applied the policy announced in *Golden Globes* in subsequent cases.

* * *

DISCUSSION

Fox, CBS, and NBC (collectively, "the Networks"), supported by several amici, raise a variety of arguments against the validity of the Remand Order [which affirmed the FCC's conclusion], including: (1) the Remand Order is arbitrary and capricious because the Commission's regulation of "fleeting expletives" represents a dramatic change in agency policy without adequate explanation; (2) the FCC's "community standards" analysis is arbitrary and meaningless; (3) the FCC's indecency findings are invalid because the Commission made no finding of scienter; (4) the FCC's definition of "profane" is contrary to law; (5) the FCC's indecency regime is unconstitutionally vague; (6) the FCC's indecency test permits the Commission to make subjective determinations about the quality of speech in violation of the First Amendment; and (7) the FCC's indecency regime is an impermissible content-based regulation of speech that violates the First Amendment. The FCC, also supported by several amici, dispute each of these contentions. We agree with the first argument advanced by the Networks, and therefore do not reach any other potential problems with the FCC's decision.

* * *

II. Administrative Procedure Act

Courts will set aside agency decisions found to be "arbitrary, capricious, an abuse of discretion, or otherwise not in accordance with law." 5 U.S.C. §706(2)(A) . . . The Networks contend that the Remand Order is arbitrary and capricious because the FCC has made a 180-degree turn regarding its treatment of "fleeting expletives" without providing a reasoned explanation justifying the about-face. We agree.

First, there is no question that the FCC has changed its policy. As outlined in detail above, prior to the *Golden Globes* decision the FCC had consistently taken the view that isolated, non-literal, fleeting expletives did not run afoul of its indecency regime. *See, e.g., Pacifica Clarification Order,* 59 F.C.C.2d 892, at ¶4 n. 1 (advising broadcasters that "it would be inequitable for us to hold a licensee responsible for indecent language" that occurred during a live broadcast without an opportunity for journalistic editing) [other citations omitted]. This consistent enforcement policy changed with the issuance of *Golden Globes* . . .

The Commission declined to issue a forfeiture in *Golden Globes* precisely because its decision represented a departure from its prior rulings. *See id.* at ¶15 ("Given, however, that Commission and staff precedent prior to our decision today *permitted the broadcast at issue,* and that we take a *new approach to profanity,* NBC and its affiliates necessarily did not have the requisite notice to justify a penalty." (emphasis added)). . . .

Agencies are of course free to revise their rules and policies. *See Chevron, U.S.A., Inc. v. Natural Res. Def. Council, Inc.,* 467 U.S. 837, 863 (1984) ("An initial agency interpretation is not instantly carved in stone."). Such a change, however, must provide a reasoned analysis for departing from prior precedent. . . . An agency's "failure to come to grips with conflicting precedent constitutes an inexcusable departure from the essential requirement of reasoned decision making." *Ramaprakash v. FAA.,* 346 F.3d 1121, 1125 (D.C.Cir.2003) (internal quotation marks omitted). Accordingly, agency action will be set aside as arbitrary and capricious if the agency fails to provide a reasoned explanation for its decision. *See, e.g., Massachusetts v. EPA,* 127 S.Ct. 1438, 1463 (2007) ("EPA has offered no reasoned explanation for its refusal to decide whether greenhouse gases cause or contribute to climate change. Its action was therefore arbitrary, capricious, . . . or otherwise not in accordance with law."); [other citations omitted].

Our evaluation of the agency's reasons for its change in policy is confined to the reasons articulated by the agency itself. [citations omitted]. The primary reason for the crackdown on fleeting expletives advanced by the FCC is the so-called "first blow" theory described in the Supreme Court's *Pacifica* decision. In *Pacifica,* the Supreme Court justified the FCC's regulation of the broadcast media in part on the basis that indecent material on the airwaves enters into the privacy of the home uninvited and without warning. 438 U.S. at 748. The Court rejected the argument that the audience could simply tune-out: "To say that one may avoid further offense by turning off the radio when he hears indecent language is like saying that the remedy for an assault is to run away after the first blow." *Id.* at 748-49. Relying on this statement in *Pacifica,* the Commission attempts to justify its stance on fleeting expletives on the basis that "granting an automatic exemption for 'isolated or fleeting' expletives unfairly forces viewers (including children) to take 'the first blow.'" *Remand Order,* at ¶25.

We cannot accept this argument as a reasoned basis justifying the Commission's new rule. First, the Commission provides no reasonable explanation for why it has changed its perception that a fleeting expletive was not a harmful "first blow" for the nearly thirty years between *Pacifica* and *Golden Globes.* More problematic, however, is that the "first blow" theory bears no rational connection to the Commission's actual policy regarding fleeting expletives. As the FCC itself stressed during oral argument in this case, the Commission does not take the position that *any* occurrence of an expletive is indecent or profane under its rules. [FN7 Such a per se ban would likely raise constitutional questions above and beyond the concerns raised by the current policy. *See Pacifica,* 438 U.S. at 746 (plurality opinion) ("Although these words ordinarily lack literary, political, or scientific value, they are not entirely outside the protection of the First Amendment. Some uses of even the most offensive words are unquestionably protected.").] For example, although "there is no outright news exemption from our indecency rules," *Remand Order,* at ¶71, the Commission will apparently excuse an expletive when it occurs during a *"bona fide* news interview," *id.* at ¶72-73 (deferring to CBS's "plausible characterization" of a segment of The Early Show interviewing a contestant on its reality show Survivor: Vanuatu as news programming and finding expletive uttered during that part of the show not indecent or profane). Certainly viewers (including children) watching the live broadcast of The Early Show were "force[d] . . . to take the 'first blow'" of the expletive uttered by the Survivor: Vanuatu contestant. . . . Thus, the record simply does not support the position that the Commission's new policy was based on its concern with the public's mere exposure to this language on the airwaves. The "first blow" theory, therefore, fails to provide the reasoned explanation necessary to justify the FCC's departure from established precedent.

The Remand Order makes passing reference to other reasons that purportedly support its change in policy, none of which we find sufficient. For instance, the Commission states that even non-literal uses of expletives fall within its indecency definition because it is "difficult (if not impossible) to distinguish whether a word is being used as an expletive or as a literal description of sexual or excretory functions." *Remand Order,* at ¶23. This defies any commonsense understanding of these words, which, as the general public well knows, are often used in everyday conversation without any "sexual or excretory" meaning. Bono's exclamation that his victory at the Golden Globe Awards was "really, really fucking brilliant" is a prime example of a non-literal use of the "F-Word" that has no sexual connotation. *See Golden Globes (Bureau Decision),* 18 F.C.C.R. 19859, at ¶5 ("As a threshold matter, the material aired during the 'Golden Globe Awards' program does not describe or depict sexual and excretory activities and organs . . . . Rather, the performer used the word 'fucking' as an adjective or expletive to emphasize an exclamation."), *rev'd by Golden Globes,* 19 F.C.C.R. 4975 (2004). Similarly, as NBC illustrates in its brief, in recent times even the top leaders of our government have used variants of these expletives in a manner that no reasonable person would believe referenced "sexual or excretory organs or activities." *See* Br. of Intervenor NBC at 31-32 & n. 3 (citing President Bush's remark to British Prime Minister Tony Blair that the United Nations needed to "get Syria to get Hezbollah to stop doing this shit" and Vice President Cheney's widely-reported "Fuck yourself" comment to Senator Patrick Leahy on the floor of the U.S. Senate).

* * *

For decades broadcasters relied on the FCC's restrained approach to indecency regulation and its consistent rejection of arguments that isolated expletives were indecent. The agency asserts the same interest in protecting children as it asserted thirty years ago, but until the *Golden Globes* decision, it had never banned fleeting expletives. While the FCC is free to change its previously settled view on this issue, it must provide a reasoned basis for that change. [citation omitted]. The FCC's decision, however, is devoid of any evidence that suggests a fleeting expletive is harmful, let alone establishes that this harm is serious enough to warrant government regulation. Such evidence would seem to be particularly relevant today when children likely hear this language far more often from other sources than they did in the 1970s when the Commission first began sanctioning indecent speech. Yet the Remand Order provides no reasoned analysis of the purported "problem" it is seeking to address with its new indecency policy from which this court can conclude that such regulation of speech is reasonable. *See, e.g., United States v. Playboy Enter. Group, Inc.,* 529 U.S. 803, 822-23 (2000) (rejecting indecency regulation of cable television in part because "[t]he question is whether an actual problem has been proved in this case. We agree that the Government has failed to establish a pervasive, nationwide problem justifying its nationwide daytime speech ban."); [other citations omitted].

* * *

Accordingly, we find that the FCC's new policy regarding "fleeting expletives" fails to provide a reasoned analysis justifying its departure from the agency's established practice. For this reason, Fox's petition for review is granted, the Remand Order is vacated, and the matter is remanded to the FCC for further proceedings consistent with this opinion. Because we have found that the FCC's new indecency regime, announced in *Golden Globes* and applied in the Remand Order, is invalid under the Administrative Procedure Act, the stay of enforcement previously granted by this court in our September 6th order is vacated as moot.

[FN: We recognize that what follows is dicta, but we note that "dicta often serve extremely valuable purposes . . . ." The Honorable Pierre N. Leval, Judging Under the Constitution: Dicta About Dicta, 81 N.Y.U. L.Rev. 1249, 1253 (2006).]

III. Constitutional Challenges

"A fundamental and longstanding principle of judicial restraint requires that courts avoid reaching constitutional questions in advance of the necessity of deciding them." *Lyng v. N.W. Indian Cemetery Protective Ass'n,* 485 U.S. 439, 445 (1988). Thus, we refrain from deciding the various constitutional challenges to the Remand Order raised by the Networks. We note, however, that in reviewing these numerous constitutional challenges, which were fully briefed to this court and discussed at length during oral argument, we are skeptical that the Commission can provide a reasoned explanation for its "fleeting expletive" regime that would pass constitutional muster. Because we doubt that the Networks will refrain from further litigation on these precise issues if, on remand, the Commission merely provides further explanation with no other changes to its policy, in the interest of judicial economy we make the following observations.

As an initial matter, we note that *all* speech covered by the FCC's indecency policy is fully protected by the First Amendment. *See Sable Commc''ns v. FCC,* 492 U.S. 115, 126 (1989) (noting that speech "which is indecent but not obscene is protected by the First Amendment");[citation omitted]. With that backdrop in mind, we question whether the FCC's indecency test can survive First Amendment scrutiny. For instance, we are sympathetic to the Networks' contention that the FCC's indecency test is undefined, indiscernible, inconsistent, and consequently, unconstitutionally vague. Although the Commission has declared that all variants of "fuck" and "shit" are presumptively indecent and profane, repeated use of those words in "Saving Private Ryan," for example, was neither indecent nor profane. And while multiple occurrences of expletives in "Saving Private Ryan" was not gratuitous, *Saving Private Ryan,* 20 F.C.C.R. 4507, at ¶14, a single occurrence of "fucking" in the Golden Globe Awards was "shocking and gratuitous," *Golden Globes,* 19 F.C.C.R. 4975, at ¶9. Parental ratings and advisories were important in finding "Saving Private Ryan" not patently offensive under contemporary community standards, *Saving Private Ryan,* 20 F.C.C.R. 4507, at ¶15, but irrelevant in evaluating a rape scene in another fictional movie, *see Omnibus Order,* 21 F.C.C.R.

2664, at ¶38 (issuing maximum forfeiture penalty against NBC Telemundo for movie "Con el Corazón en la Mano"). The use of numerous expletives was "integral" to a fictional movie about war, *Saving Private Ryan,* 20 F.C.C.R. 4507, at ¶14, but occasional expletives spoken by real musicians were indecent and profane because the educational purpose of the documentary "could have been fulfilled and all viewpoints expressed without the repeated broadcast of expletives," *Omnibus* Order, 21 F.C.C.R. 2664, at ¶82 (finding Martin Scorsese's PBS documentary "The Blues: Godfathers and Sons" indecent). The "S-Word" on The Early Show was not indecent because it was in the context of a "*bona fide* news interview," but "there is no outright news exemption from our indecency rules," *Remand Order,* at ¶¶68, 71-73. We can understand why the Networks argue that FCC's "patently offensive as measured by contemporary community standards" indecency test coupled with its "artistic necessity" exception fails to provide the clarity required by the Constitution, creates an undue chilling effect on free speech, and requires broadcasters to "steer far wider of the unlawful zone," *Speiser v. Randall,* 357 U.S. 513, 526 (1958).

The Networks' position is further buttressed by the Supreme Court's decision in *Reno v. ACLU,* 521 U.S. 844 (1997), which struck down as unconstitutionally vague a similarly-worded indecency regulation of the Internet. The Court found that the statute's use of the "general, undefined terms 'indecent' and 'patently offensive' cover large amounts of nonpornographic material with serious educational or other value. Moreover, the 'community standards' criterion as applied to the Internet means that any communication available to a nation wide audience will be judged by the standards of the community most likely to be offended by the message." *Id.* at 877-78. Because of the "vague contours" of the regulation, the Court held that "it unquestionably silences some speakers whose messages would be entitled to constitutional protection," and thus violated the First Amendment. *Id.* at 874. Because *Reno* holds that a regulation that covers speech that "in context, depicts or describes, in terms patently offensive as measured by contemporary community standards, sexual or excretory activities or organs" is unconstitutionally vague, we are skeptical that the FCC's identically-worded indecency test could nevertheless provide the requisite clarity to withstand constitutional scrutiny. Indeed, we are hard pressed to imagine a regime that is more vague than one that relies entirely on consideration of the otherwise unspecified "context" of a broadcast indecency.

*   *   *

Finally, we recognize there is some tension in the law regarding the appropriate level of First Amendment scrutiny. In general, restrictions on First Amendment liberties prompt courts to apply strict scrutiny. *FCC v. League of Women Voters,* 468 U.S. 364, 376 (1984). Outside the broadcasting context, the Supreme Court has consistently applied strict scrutiny to indecency regulations. *See, e.g., Playboy,* 529 U.S. at 811-813 (holding that regulation proscribing indecent content on cable television was content-based restriction of speech subject to strict scrutiny); *Sable,* 492 U.S. at 126 (holding that indecency regulation of telephone messages was content-based restriction subject to strict scrutiny); *Reno,* 521 U.S. at 868 (holding that indecency regulation of Internet was a content-based restriction subject to strict scrutiny). At the same time, however, the Supreme Court has also considered broadcast media exceptional. "[B]ecause broadcast regulation involves unique considerations, our cases . . . have never gone so far as to demand that such regulations serve 'compelling' governmental interests." *League of Women Voters,* 468 U.S. at 376. Restrictions on broadcast "speech" have been upheld "when we [are] satisfied that the restriction is narrowly tailored to further a substantial governmental interest." *Id.* at 380.

The Networks contend that the bases for treating broadcast media "different[ly]" have "eroded over time," particularly because 86 percent of American households now subscribe to cable or satellite services, *Remand Order,* at ¶49. As the Networks argue, this and other realities have "eviscerated" the notion that broadcast content is, as it was termed in *Pacifica,* 438 U.S. at 748-49, "uniquely pervasive" and "uniquely accessible to children." Whatever merit these arguments may have, they cannot sway us in light of Supreme Court precedent. *See, e.g., Reno,* 521 U.S. at 867 (noting that "as a matter of history" broadcast television has enjoyed less First Amendment protection than other media, including the internet); *Pacifica,* 438 U.S. at 748-50.

Nevertheless, we would be remiss not to observe that it is increasingly difficult to describe the broadcast media as uniquely pervasive and uniquely accessible to children, and at some point in the future, strict scrutiny may properly apply in the context of regulating broadcast television. In light of this possibility, the Networks rightly rest their constitutional argument in part on the holding of *Playboy,* which involved a challenge to a statute requiring cable operators who provide channels primarily dedicated to sexually explicit or otherwise indecent programming to either fully scramble these channels or limit their transmission to the 10pm to 6am safe harbor period. 529 U.S. at 806. The Supreme Court, applying strict scrutiny, invalidated the statute because a less restrictive alternative to the prohibition existed: "One plausible, less restrictive alternative could be found in another section of the [Telecommunications] Act [of 1996]: §504, which requires a cable operator, 'upon request by a cable service subscriber . . . without charge, [to] fully scramble or otherwise fully block' any channel the subscriber does not wish to receive." *Id.* at 809-10. The Court held: This "targeted blocking is less restrictive than banning, and the Government cannot ban speech if targeted blocking is a feasible and effective means of furthering its compelling interests." *Id.* at 815. In so holding, the Court suggested its decision might go beyond the mechanistic application of strict scrutiny, and rely in part on a notional pillar of free speech-namely, choice:

[Reversal of the FCC's construction of "profane" omitted]

CONCLUSION

As the foregoing indicates, we are doubtful that by merely proffering a reasoned analysis for its new approach to indecency and profanity, the Commission can adequately respond to the constitutional and statutory challenges raised by the Networks. Nevertheless, because we can decide this case on this narrow ground, we vacate and remand so that the Commission can set forth that analysis. While we fully expect the Networks to raise the same arguments they have raised to this court if the Commission does nothing more on remand than provide additional explanation for its departure from prior precedent, we can go no further in this opinion. Accordingly, we grant the petition for review, vacate the order of the FCC, and remand the case for further proceedings consistent with this opinion. The stay previously granted by this court is vacated as moot.

LEVAL, J., dissenting.

I respectfully dissent from my colleagues' ruling because I believe the Federal Communications Commission ("FCC" or "Commission") gave a reasoned explanation for its change of standard and thus complied with the requirement of the Administrative Procedures Act, 5 U.S.C. §706(2)(A).

* * *

The occurrences under review in this case followed soon after the Bono incident, during live broadcasts by Fox of Billboard Music Awards shows in 2002 and 2003. In the 2002 Billboard Music Awards, the actress and singer Cher, expressing triumphant delight upon her receipt of an award, said, "People have been telling me I'm on the way out every year, right? So fuck 'em." The incident during the 2003 Billboard Music Awards involved Nicole Richie and Paris Hilton, the co-stars of a serialized televised comedy show entitled, "The Simple Life," as presenters of awards. In "The Simple Life," Richie and Hilton play themselves as two spoiled, rich young women from Beverly Hills who cope with life on a farm. In joking reference to their own show, Richie said, "Why do they even call it 'The Simple Life?' Have you ever tried to get cow shit out of a Prada purse? It's not so fucking simple." The Commission received complaints about each incident. Referring to its newly changed policy developed in response to the Bono incident in *Golden Globes,* the Commission found that the two Billboard Music incidents were violations. *See Complaints Regarding Various Television Broadcasts Between February 2, 2002 and March 8, 2005,* 21 F.C.C.R. 13299 (2006) ("*Remand Order* "). Fox brought this action seeking to invalidate the Commission's rulings.

In adjudicating indecency complaints the Commission generally employs a context-based evaluation to determine whether the particular utterance is "*patently offensive* as measured by contemporary community standards." *Industry Guidance on the Commission's Case Law Interpreting 18 U.S.C. §1464,* 16 F.C.C.R. 7999, at ¶¶8 (2001) ("*Industry Guidance* ") (emphasis in original). Factors weighing in favor of a finding of indecency are: "(1) the *explicitness or graphic nature* of the description or depiction of sexual or excretory organs or activities; (2) whether the material *dwells on or repeats at length* descriptions of sexual or excretory organs or activities; (3) *whether the material appears to pander or is used to titillate,* or *whether the material appears to have been presented for its shock value." Industry Guidance,* at ¶¶10 (emphasis in original). Especially in relation to the "pandering" factor, a finding of violation is less likely if the broadcast of the utterance involved a genuine news report, or if censorship of the expletive would harm or distort artistic integrity. Prior to the Bono incident, the Commission attached great importance to the second factor, which focuses on whether an expletive was repeated. Under the pre-*Golden Globes* rulings, the fact that an utterance was fleeting was virtually conclusive in assuring it would not be deemed a violation (unless it breached special barriers, such as by referring to sexual activities with children). With its *Golden Globes* adjudication, however, the Commission adopted a less permissive stance. It announced that henceforth fleeting expletives would be judged according to a standard more closely aligned with repeated utterances of expletives. Thus, the Commission has declared that it remains unlikely to find a violation in an expletive that is broadcast in the context of a genuine news report, or where censorship by bleeping out the expletive would compromise artistic integrity, but it will no longer give a nearly automatic pass merely because the expletive was not repeated. *See Remand Order,* at ¶23.

The Commission explained succinctly why lack of repetition of the F-Word would no longer result in a virtual free pass. "[W]e believe that, given the core-meaning of the 'F-Word,' any use of that word or a variation, in any context, inherently has a sexual connotation. . . . The 'F-Word' is one of the most vulgar, graphic and explicit descriptions of sexual activity in the English language. Its use invariably invokes a coarse sexual image." *Golden Globes,* at ¶¶8-9. "[A]ny use of that word has a sexual connotation even if the word is not used literally." *Remand Order,* at ¶16.

My colleagues find that in so altering its standards the Commission has acted illegally. They rule that the Commission failed to give a reasoned analysis explaining the change of rule. They accordingly find that the change of standard was arbitrary and capricious and therefore violated the Administrative Procedure Act. I disagree. In explanation of this relatively modest change of standard, the Commission gave a sensible, although not necessarily compelling, reason. In relation to the word "fuck," the Commission's central explanation for the change was essentially its perception that the "F-Word" is not only of extreme and graphic vulgarity, but also conveys an inescapably sexual connotation. The Commission thus concluded that the use of the F-Word-even in a single fleeting instance without repetition-is likely to constitute an offense to the decency standards of §1464.

The standards for judicial review of administrative actions are discussed in a few leading Supreme Court opinions from which the majority quotes. Agencies operate with broad discretionary power to establish rules and standards, and courts are required to give deference to agency decisions. *See Chevron U.S.A., Inc. v. Natural Res. Def. Council, Inc.,* 467 U.S. 837, 844 (1984). A court must not "substitute its judgment for that of the agency." *Motor Vehicle Mfrs. Ass'n of U.S., Inc. v. State Farm Mut. Auto. Ins. Co.,* 463 U.S. 29, 43 (1983); *see also Vermont Yankee Nuclear Power Corp. v. Natural Res. Def. Council, Inc.,* 435 U.S. 519, 558 (1978) ("Administrative decisions should [not] be set aside . . . because the court is unhappy with the result reached."). In general, an agency's determination will be upheld by a court unless found to be "arbitrary and capricious." *See* 5 U.S.C. 706(2)(A).

An agency is free furthermore to change its standards. *See Chevron,* 467 U.S. at 863 ("An initial agency interpretation is not instantly carved in stone."); [other citations omitted]. If an agency without explanation were to make an adjudication which is not consistent with the agency's previously established standards, the troubling question would arise whether the agency has lawfully changed its standard, or whether it has arbitrarily failed to adhere to its standard, which it may not lawfully do. Accordingly, our court has ruled that "an agency . . . cannot simply adopt inconsistent positions without presenting 'some reasoned analysis.'" *Huntington Hosp.,* 319 F.3d at 79. . . .

In my view, in changing its position on the repetition of an expletive, the Commission complied with these requirements. It made clear acknowledgment that its *Golden Globes* and *Remand Order* rulings were not consistent with its prior standard regarding lack of repetition. It announced the adoption of a new standard. And it furnished a reasoned explanation for the change. Although one can reasonably disagree with the Commission's new position, its explanation-at least with respect to the F-Word-is not irrational, arbitrary, or capricious. The Commission thus satisfied the standards of the Administrative Procedures Act.

The Commission explained that the F-Word is "one of the most vulgar, graphic and explicit descriptions of sexual activity in the English language [whose] use invariably invokes a coarse sexual image." *Golden Globes,* at ¶9. In other words, the Commission found, contrary to its earlier policy, that the word is of such graphic explicitness in inevitable reference to sexual activity that absence of repetition does not save it from violating the standard of decency.

My colleagues offer several arguments in support of their conclusion that the Commission's explanation was not reasonable and therefore arbitrary and capricious. They argue (i) the Commission's position is irrational because of inconsistency resulting from the Commission's willingness to allow viewers to be subjected to a "first blow" if it comes in the context of a genuine news broadcast; (ii) the Commission's prediction that allowance of fleeting expletives will result in a great increase in their incidence is irrational because prior experience was to the contrary; and (iii) the Commission is "divorced from reality" believing that the F-Word invariably invokes a sexual connotation. I respectfully disagree.

* * *

[W]hile the Commission will indeed allow the broadcast of the same material in some circumstances but not in others, I do not see why this differentiation should be considered irrational. It rather seeks to reconcile conflicting values. On the one hand, it recognizes, as stressed by the Supreme Court in *Pacifica,* the potential for harm to children resulting from exposure to indecency. On the other hand, the Commission has historically recognized that categorical prohibition of the broadcast of all instances of usage of a word generally considered indecent would suppress material of value, which should not be deemed indecent upon consideration of the context. This is not irrationality. It is an attempt on the part of the Commission over the years to reconcile conflicting values through standards which take account of context.

The majority then argues that the Commission reasoned irrationally when in its *Remand Order,* as a part of its explanation for its change of position, the Commission observed:

> [G]ranting an automatic exemption for "isolated or fleeting" expletives . . . would as a matter of logic permit broadcasters to air expletives at all hours of a day so long as they did so one at a time. For example, broadcasters would be able to air . . . offensive . . . words, regardless of context, with impunity . . . provided that they did not air more than one expletive in any program segment.

Remand Order, at ¶25. The majority asserts that this concern was "divorced from reality." Majority op. at page 27. On the majority's view, because broadcasters did not "barrage[ ] the airwaves with expletives" during the period prior to *Golden Globes* when fleeting expletives received a free pass, they would not do so in the future.

The agency has one prediction of what would likely occur in the future under the pre-*Golden Globes* policy. The majority has another. The majority may be right in speculating that the Commission's concern is exaggerated. Who knows? As a matter of law, it makes no difference. The court is obligated to give deference to agency judgment and may not substitute its judgment for that of the agency, or set aside an agency action merely because the court believes the agency is wrong. [citations omitted].

Furthermore, if obligated to choose, I would bet my money on the agency's prediction. The majority's view presupposes that the future would repeat the past. It argues that because the networks were not flooded with discrete, fleeting expletives when fleeting expletives had a free pass, they would not be flooded in the future. This fails to take account of two facts. First, the words proscribed by the Commission's decency standards are much more common in daily discourse today than they were thirty years ago. Second, the regulated networks compete for audience with the unregulated cable channels, which increasingly make liberal use of their freedom to fill programming with such expletives. The media press regularly reports how difficult it is for networks to compete with cable for that reason. It seems to me the agency has good reason to expect that a marked increase would occur if the old policy were continued.

In any event, even if the majority could reasonably label *this aspect* of the Commission's reasoning "arbitrary and capricious," it still would not matter. The agency's action in changing the standard for fleeting expletives did not depend on the defensibility of this prediction. It is at most a small part of the agency's justification for its action.

Finally the majority disagrees with the Commission's view that the word "fuck" communicates an "inherently . . . sexual connotation [and] invariably invokes a coarse sexual image." *Golden Globes,* at ¶¶8-9. The majority notes that the F-Word is often used in everyday conversation without any sexual meaning. I agree with the majority that the word is often used without a necessary *intention on the part of the speaker* to refer to sex. A student who gets a disappointing grade on a test, a cook who burns the roast, or a driver who returns to his parked car to find a parking ticket on the windshield, might holler out the F-Word to express anger or disappointment. The word is also sometimes used to express delight, as with Bono's exhilarated utterance on his receipt of his award. Some use it more as a declaration of uncompromising toughness, or of alignment on the side of vulgarity against prissy manners, without necessarily intending to evoke any sexual meaning. Some use it to intensify whatever it is they may be saying, and some sprinkle the word indiscriminately throughout their conversation with no apparent meaning whatsoever.

The majority, however, misunderstands the Commission's reasoning, or in any event interprets it in the manner least favorable to the Commission. In observing that *fuck* "invariably invokes a coarse sexual image," *Golden Globes,* at ¶9, that this is so "even if the word is not used literally," *Remand Order,* at ¶16, and that its power to offend "derives from its sexual . . . meaning," *id.* at ¶23, the Commission did not mean that every speaker who utters the word invariably intends to communicate an offensive sexual meaning. The Commission explicitly recognized that the word can be used in a manner that does not intend a sexual meaning. A fairer reading of the Commission's meaning is that, even when the speaker does not intend a sexual meaning, a substantial part of the community, and of the television audience, will understand the word as freighted with an offensive sexual connotation. It is surely not irrational for the Commission to conclude that, according to the understanding of a substantial segment of the community, the F-Word is never completely free of an offensive, sexual connotation. It is no accident that in many languages, the equivalent of the F-Word finds usage, as in English, to express anger, disgust, insult, and confrontation.

What we have is at most a difference of opinion between a court and an agency. Because of the deference courts must give to the reasoning of a duly authorized administrative agency in matters within the agency's competence, a court's disagreement with the Commission on this question is of no consequence. The Commission's position is not irrational; it is not arbitrary and capricious.

I believe that in changing its standard, the Commission furnished a reasoned explanation, and thus satisfied the requirements of the Administrative Procedures Act. I therefore respectfully dissent.

NOTES AND QUESTIONS

1.   **What We Have Here is A Difference of Opinion.** Judge Leval claims that the majority opinion fails to accord proper respect to the judgment of an expert agency. To what extent does the subject of this case—the interpretation of the word "fuck" as opposed to, say, appropriate rules governing interference between adjacent spectrum licensees—affect the level of deference accorded to the Commission? Is that appropriate?

2.   **The First Amendment Backdrop.** The nominal subject of the case is an administrative law question about whether the FCC acted in an irrational manner in changing its policy. But as the unusual step of discussing the First Amendment issue at length in dicta suggests, there is a lurking First Amendment challenge. Is the Second Circuit's discussion of this issue, which was wholly unnecessary to its ruling, appropriate? Why did the court discuss the issue?

3.   **Next Stop: The Supreme Court?** The FCC's increased crackdown on indecency and its judgment that "fuck" communicates an "inherently . . . sexual connotation [and] invariably

invokes a coarse sexual image" may be ultimately reviewed by the Supreme Court. Any such review will beg the question as to whether (1) the indecency standard is "void for vagueness" because it cannot provide fair warning to regulated parties; and (2) the First Amendment continues to provide broadcasters with a lower level of protection. Notably, however, the Supreme Court could not reach either of these questions—which were at the core of *Pacifica*—unless it held that the FCC properly changed its attitude on the meaning of "fuck" and whether a single utterance of the word is indecent.

4.   What Now? If you represented a group that wanted to keep indecency off the airwaves, what would you recommend they advocate? Push the FCC to do a better job of articulating their reasons for their policy on "fuck" and "shit"? But what more could the FCC say? And if the FCC did overcome the administrative law problem, or if Congress eliminated the administrative law problem by specifically authorizing the FCC to penalize all iterations of "fuck" and "shit," then the First Amendment issue would be squarely raised. For advocates of indecency regulation, is a judicial ruling on the First Amendment issues desirable? Inevitable? Would you instead push for alternatives to direct regulation, such as enhancements to the V-chip (see the next section of the casebook)?

Before §5.5 on p. 306, insert:

In 2007, the FCC issued a report based on its Notice of Inquiry referenced in notes 1 and 6 above. This report highlights its grave concerns as to availability of violent programming on TV and calls upon Congress to grant it jurisdiction to extend its oversight of "indecent" programming to matters involving not merely content of a sexual nature, but violent content as well. An excerpt of this report is set forth below.

**Violent Television Programming and its Impact on Children
Report, FCC -7-50, 2007 WL 1224879 (April 25, 2007)**

I.   INTRODUCTION

1.   Television is an integral part of the lives of American families. An average American household has the television set turned on 8 hours and 11 minutes daily, and children watch on average between two and four hours of television every day. Depending on their age, one to two thirds of children have televisions in their bedrooms. By the time most children begin the first grade, they will have spent the equivalent of three school years in front of the television set.

2.   Violent content in television programming has been a matter of private and governmental concern and discussion almost from the beginning of television broadcasting. A broad range of television programming aired today contains such content, including, for example, cartoons, dramatic series, professional sports such as boxing, news coverage, and nature programs. The public is concerned about the amount of violent television programming available to children, with many urging action to restrict such content.

3.   It is within this context that the Commission received a request from thirty-nine members of the U.S. House of Representatives asking us to undertake an inquiry on television violence. In response, the Commission issued a *Notice of Inquiry* ("*NOI*") in this proceeding, seeking public input on a variety of matters tied to the issue of violent television content. The Commission has received hundreds of filings from interested parties and individuals.

4.   The House members asked the Commission to solicit comment on three essential issues:

- What are the negative effects on children caused by the cumulative viewing of excessively violent programming?

- What are the constitutional limits on the government's ability to restrict the broadcast of excessively violent programming when children are likely to be a significant or substantial part of the viewing audience? In particular, could television violence regulations, including possible time channeling requirements, be narrowly tailored to the governmental interests they are intended to serve?

- Is it in the public interest for the government to adopt a definition of "excessively violent programming that is harmful to children," and could the government formulate and implement such a definition in a constitutional manner?

    5.   *Summary.* In the *NOI*, the Commission sought comment on the relationship between media violence and aggression in children. In this *Report*, we find that there is deep concern among many American parents and health professionals regarding harm from viewing violence in media. We also agree with the views of the Surgeon General that there is strong evidence that exposure to violence in the media can increase aggressive behavior in children, at least in the short term. In the *NOI*, the Commission sought comment on proposals aimed at regulating violent television content, such as a "safe harbor" period similar to the one in place for indecent broadcast content. In this *Report*, we recognize that violent content is a protected form of speech under the First Amendment, but note that the government interests at stake, such as protecting children from excessively violent television programming, are similar to those which have been found to justify other content-based regulations. In the *NOI*, the Commission asked questions concerning the adequacy of current program blocking technology and the effectiveness of the TV ratings system in helping parents control access to violent programming. In this *Report*, we find that although the V-chip and TV ratings system appear useful in the abstract, they are not effective at protecting children from violent content for a number of reasons. In particular, we find that the TV ratings system has certain weaknesses that prevent parents from screening out much programming that they find objectionable. In the *NOI*, the Commission asked how the government might define "violence" for regulatory purposes. In this *Report*, we recognize the difficulties associated with drafting a concise and legally sustainable definition of violence for regulatory purposes, but we suggest an approach that Congress may want to consider in crafting a definition. Finally, we note our conclusion that, given the findings in this report, action should be taken to address violent programming and suggest that Congress could implement a time-channeling solution that would more effectively protect children from violent programming and/or mandate other forms of consumer choice that would better support parents' efforts to safeguard their children from exposure to violent programming.

II.   THE EFFECTS OF VIEWING VIOLENT TELEVISION PROGRAMMING ON CHILDREN

    6.   We agree with the views of the Surgeon General and find that, on balance, research provides strong evidence that exposure to violence in the media can increase aggressive behavior in children, at least in the short term. Over the course of several decades, considerable research has been undertaken to examine television's impact on children's learning and behavior. Three types of studies are generally described in the literature: (1) field experiments in which subjects are shown video programming and their short-term post-viewing behavior is monitored by researchers; (2) cross-sectional studies involving samples of individuals whose conduct is correlated with the amount and type of their television viewing; and (3) longitudinal studies that

survey the same group of individuals at different times over many years to determine the effects of television viewing on subsequent behavior. Through these studies, scholars have attempted to establish a cause-and-effect relationship between viewing violent content and subsequent aggression in children.

7.   The researchers have focused on three possible harmful effects: (1) increased antisocial behavior, including imitations of aggression or negative interactions with others, (2) increased desensitization to violence, and (3) increased fear of becoming a victim of violence. Researchers have theorized that children's viewing of violent television programming may affect later behavior in three ways: (1) through observing schemas about a hostile world, (2) through scripts for social problem solving that focus on aggression, and (3) through normative beliefs that aggression is acceptable. Alternatively, exposure to violent programming may desensitize the child's innate negative emotional response to violence, thus making aggressive acts easier to commit or tolerate While the Commission sought evidence relating to such research, very little new information on the issue was submitted into the record of this proceeding.

8.   Some studies find evidence of a cause-and-effect relationship between viewing televised violence by children and aggression or other changes in the behavior of the children on both a short-term and a longer-term basis. For example, Craig Anderson, a professor and former chair of the Psychology Department at Iowa State University who has conducted and published numerous "media harms" studies, asserts that research on violent television, films, video games, and music reveals "unequivocal evidence" that media violence increases the likelihood of aggressive and violent behavior in both immediate and long-term contexts. . . .

9.   Joanne Cantor, a professor at the University of Wisconsin-Madison, concurs and states that her research has found that children show higher levels of hostility after exposure to media violence - ranging from being in a "nasty mood" to an increased tendency to interpret a neutral comment or action as an attack. . . .

10.   The *Notice of Inquiry* in this proceeding referenced two recent significant efforts to summarize the state of the evidence regarding the effects of televised violence on children. A review of the scientific research, which appears as part of the Federal Trade Commission's report on *Marketing Violent Entertainment to Children,* summarized the research as follows:

> A majority of the investigations into the impact of media violence on children find that there is a high *correlation* between exposure to media violence and aggressive and at times violent behavior. In addition, a number of research efforts report that exposure to media violence is correlated with increased acceptance of violent behavior in others, as well as an exaggerated perception of the amount of violence in society. Regarding *causation*, however, the studies appear to be less conclusive. Most researchers and investigators agree that exposure to media violence alone does not cause a child to commit a violent act, and that it is not the sole, or even necessarily the most important, factor contributing to youth aggression, anti-social attitudes, and violence. Although a consensus among researchers exists regarding the empirical relationships, significant differences remain over the interpretation of these associations and their implications for public policy.

Others agree that while studies show a correlation, a clear causal link has not been conclusively proven. More recently, researchers at Boston Children's Hospital report that violent shows might teach and encourage aggressive behavior in children, which in turn isolates them from their peers. Like the *FTC Report*, the study shows a correlation, but does not prove causation.

16.   Others argue, however, that children are not necessarily harmed by exposure to television violence or that the research on the topic is flawed or inconclusive.   The Media Coalition, a group of trade associations representing book and magazine publishers, along with movie, recording and video manufacturers and retailers, disputes that research supports the conclusion that violence in the media causes actual violence.   In support of this view, they contend that the existing research is inconclusive and that there is no correlation between media violence and actual crime statistics.   The Media Associations, a group consisting of advertising, broadcast, and television production entities, have examined the studies on media violence and assert that the literature does not support either the claim of a causal relationship between media violence and aggression or the proposition that exposure to violent media leads to desensitization. The Media Associations assert that research findings often are mischaracterized, and, in some cases, reach conclusions that are the opposite of what has been reported.   To support their claims, the Media Associations note that Jonathan Freedman, a professor at the University of Toronto and critic of the media violence cause-and-effect theory, conducted a comprehensive review of all of the available research on this topic and concluded that "evidence does not support the hypothesis that exposure to film or television violence causes children or adults to be aggressive."

20.   Given the totality of the record before us, we agree with the view of the Surgeon General that: "a diverse body of research provides strong evidence that exposure to violence in the media can increase children's aggressive behavior in the short term."   At the same time, we do recognize that "many questions remain regarding the short- and long-term effects of media violence, especially on violent behavior."   We note that a significant number of health professionals, parents and members of the general public are concerned about television violence and its effects on children.

III.   LAW AND POLICY ADDRESSING THE DISTRIBUTION OF VIOLENT TELEVISION PROGRAMMING

21.   Members of Congress asked the Commission to address the government's authority, consistent with the First Amendment, to restrict the broadcast or other distribution of excessively violent programming and what measures to constrain or regulate such programming are most likely to be sustained in court.   Accordingly, we discuss below regulatory alternatives for protecting children from violent television content.   We begin, however, with a brief overview of the relevant constitutional framework.

22.   Violent speech and depictions of violence have been found by the courts to be protected by the First Amendment.   However, "each medium of expression presents special First Amendment problems," with broadcasting historically receiving "the most limited First Amendment protection." *FCC v. Pacifica Foundation*, 438 U.S. 726, 744 (1978).   Thus, even when broadcast speech "lies at the heart of First Amendment protection," the government may regulate it so long as its interest in doing so is "substantial" and the restriction is "narrowly tailored" to further that interest. *FCC v. League of Women Voters*, 468 U.S. 364, 380-81 (1984) While a restriction on the content of protected speech will generally be upheld only if it satisfies strict scrutiny, meaning that the restriction must further a compelling government interest and be the least restrictive means to further that interest, this exacting standard does not apply to the regulation of broadcast speech.

23.   In the realm of indecency, the U.S. Supreme Court has identified two principal reasons for the reduced First Amendment protection afforded to broadcasting: first, its "uniquely pervasive presence in the lives of all Americans;" and second, its accessibility to children,

coupled with the government's interests in the well-being of children and in supporting parental supervision of children. *Pacifica*, 438 U.S. at 748-50, *citing Ginsberg v. New York*, 390 U.S. 629 (1968). In light of these characteristics, the Court, in *Pacifica*, upheld the Commission's authority to regulate the broadcast of indecent material. Relying on *Pacifica*, the U.S. Court of Appeals for the District of Columbia Circuit later concluded in *ACT III* that the "channeling" of indecent content to the hours between 10:00 p.m. and 6:00 a.m. would not unduly burden First Amendment rights. It held that such regulation would promote the government's "compelling interest in supporting parental supervision of what children see and hear on the public airwaves." It also noted that it is "evident beyond the need for elaboration" that the government's "interest in safeguarding the physical and psychological well-being of a minor is compelling." In addition, in light of relevant U.S. Supreme Court precedent, the D.C. Circuit refused in *ACT III* to insist on scientific evidence that indecent content harms children, concluding that the government's interest in the well-being of minors is not "limited to protecting them from clinically measurable injury."

24.   *Time Channeling.* As stated above, members of Congress asked the Commission to address possible measures to protect children from excessively violent television content. We begin by discussing time channeling restrictions that would restrict such programming to hours when children are less likely to be in the viewing audience. We note that commenters disagreed about the constitutionality of such requirements. Pappas argued that they would be likely to pass constitutional muster because the government interests are substantially the same as those at stake in regulating broadcast indecency. Other commenters maintain that such requirements would be unconstitutional and unworkable.

25.   After carefully evaluating these comments and relevant precedent, we find that Congress could impose time channeling restrictions on excessively violent television programming in a constitutional manner. Just as the government has a compelling interest in protecting children from sexually explicit programming, a strong argument can be made, for the reasons discussed in Section II above, that the government also has a compelling interest in protecting children from violent programming and supporting parental supervision of minors' viewing of violent programming. We also believe that, if properly defined, excessively violent programming, like indecent programming, occupies a relatively low position in the hierarchy of First Amendment values because it is of "'slight social value as a step to truth.'" *Pacifica*, 438 U.S. at 746, *quoting Chaplinsky*, 315 U.S. at 572. Such programming is entitled to reduced First Amendment protection because of its pervasiveness and accessibility to children pursuant to the U.S. Supreme Court's reasoning in *Pacifica*.

26.   To be sure, the government, when imposing time channeling, would have to show that such regulation is a narrowly tailored means of vindicating its interests in promoting parental supervision and protecting children. In this regard, however, we note that while the alternative measures discussed below—viewer-initiated blocking and mandatory ratings—would impose lesser burdens on protected speech, we are skeptical that they will fully serve the government's interests in promoting parental supervision and protecting the well-being of minors. In addition to these measures, as discussed below, another way of providing consumers greater control—and therefore greater ability to avoid violent programming—could be to require video channels to be offered on an "a la carte" basis. As the D.C. Circuit has noted in the context of indecency: "It is fanciful to believe that the vast majority of parents who wish to shield their children from indecent material can effectively do so without meaningful restrictions on the airing of broadcast indecency." *ACT III*, 58 F.3d at 663. To cite just some of the relevant data, 81 percent of children ages two through seven sometimes watch television without adult supervision, and 91 percent of children ages four through six have turned on the television by themselves. In addition, as discussed below, the studies and surveys conducted to date tend to show that

blocking technologies and the associated TV ratings system are of limited effectiveness in supporting parental supervision of minors' viewing habits.

28.   *Viewer-Initiated Blocking* and *Mandatory Ratings*.   Besides time channeling, another possible means of protecting children from violent television content is to strengthen mechanisms that enable viewer-initiated blocking of such content. In 1996, Congress amended Title III of the Communications Act to require the incorporation of blocking technology into television sets. As of January 1, 2000, all television sets manufactured in the United States or shipped in interstate commerce with a picture screen of thirteen inches or larger must be equipped with a "V-chip" system that can be programmed to block violent, sexual, or other programming that parents do not wish their children to view.   However, out of a total universe of 280 million sets in U.S. households, only about 119 million sets in use today, or less than half, are equipped with V-chips.

29.   Based on the studies and surveys conducted to date, we believe that the evidence clearly points to one conclusion: the V-chip is of limited effectiveness in protecting children from violent television content.   In order for V-chip technology to block a specific category of television programming, such as violent content, it must be activated. However, many parents do not even know if the television sets in their households incorporate this technology and, of those who do, many do not use it. In 2004, the Kaiser Family Foundation conducted a telephone survey of 1,001 parents of children ages 2-17. The results showed: (1) only 15 percent of all parents have used the V-chip; (2) 26 percent of all parents have not bought a new television set since January 2000 (when the V-chip was first required in *all* sets); (3) 39 percent of parents have bought a new television set since January 2000, but do not think it includes a V-chip; and (4) 20 percent of parents know they have a V-chip, but have not used it. According to a 2003 study, parents' low level of V-chip use is explained in part by parents' unawareness of the device and the "multi-step and often confusing process" necessary to use it.   Only 27 percent of parents in the study group could figure out how to program the V-Chip, and many parents "who might otherwise have used the V-Chip were frustrated by an inability to get it to work properly." A March 2007 Zogby poll indicates, among other things, that 88 percent of respondents did not use a V-chip or cable box parental controls in the previous week, leading the Parents Television Council to call the television industry's V-chip education campaign "a failure."

30.   In addition to mandating inclusion of V-chip technology in television sets, the Act provides cable subscribers with some ways to block unwanted programming.   These provisions of the Act, however, do not benefit households receiving their television programming via over-the-air broadcasting or satellite. Further, similar to the V-chip, to take advantage of these measures a cable subscriber first must be aware of and then affirmatively request that such measures be employed. Finally, to receive these protections, a cable subscriber must take several steps and incur some costs.

32.   We believe that further action to enable viewer-initiated blocking of violent television content would serve the government's interests in protecting the well-being of children and facilitating parental supervision and would be reasonably likely to be upheld as constitutional.   As indicated above, however, reliance on blocking technology alone would probably not fulfill the government's interest in protecting the well-being of children. Blocking technology does not ensure that children are prevented from viewing violent programming unless it is activated, and courts have recognized the practical limits of parental supervision.

33.   In addition, any successful viewer-initiated blocking regime with respect to violent programming would depend upon the adoption and successful implementation of an effective ratings system.   Currently, to facilitate operation of the V-chip and other blocking mechanisms, broadcast, cable, and satellite television providers, on a voluntary basis, rate

programming using the industry-devised TV ratings system guidelines and encode programs accordingly. Most television programming, except for news and sports programming, carries an age-based TV rating set by program networks and producers, and most include content-based ratings as well.

34.   Studies and surveys demonstrate, however, that the voluntary TV ratings system is of limited effectiveness in protecting children from violent television content. In the 2004 Kaiser survey discussed above, 50 percent of all parents surveyed stated that they have used the TV ratings. But about 4 in 10 parents (39 percent) stated that most programs are not rated accurately, and many parents did not fully understand what the various ratings categories mean. For example, only 24 percent of parents of young children (two-six years old) could name any of the ratings that would apply to programming appropriate for children that age. Only 12 percent of parents knew that the rating FV ("fantasy violence") is related to violent content, while 8 percent thought it meant "family viewing." One in five (20 percent) parents said that they had never heard of the TV ratings system, an increase from 14 percent in 2000 and 2001. A more recent survey indicates that only 8 percent of respondents could correctly identify the categories.

37.   To address these issues, Congress could seek to establish a mandatory ratings system that would address the shortcomings of the current system set forth above. Such a system could be defended on the grounds that it merely requires the disclosure of truthful information about a potentially harmful product (violent television programming), thereby advancing the compelling government interests without significantly burdening First Amendment rights. It could also be defended as a necessary predicate for the operation of a successful system of viewer-initiated blocking. As stated above, however, although mandatory television ratings would impose lesser burdens on protected speech, we believe the evidence demonstrates that they would not fully serve the government's interest in the well-being of minors given the limits of parental supervision recognized by the D.C. Circuit in *ACT III*. Experience also leads us to question whether such a ratings system would ever be sufficiently accurate given the myriad of practical difficulties that would accompany any comprehensive effort to ensure the accuracy of ratings. Moreover, such a requirement may have an unintended practical consequence. There is some evidence that TV ratings may actually serve to attract certain underage viewers to programming that is violent or is otherwise labeled as not intended for a child audience.

IV.   DEFINING VIOLENT OR EXCESSIVELY OR GRATUITOUSLY VIOLENT PROGRAMMING

38.   Members of Congress asked the Commission to address whether it would be in the public interest to adopt a definition of "excessively violent programming harmful to children" and to consider the constitutional limitations on the government's ability to formulate and implement such a definition. While developing a definition would be challenging, we believe that Congress could do so.

39.   Several considerations are relevant to the adoption of a definition, including the regulatory function of the definition. A definition used for TV ratings purposes might be based on different criteria than a definition used for identifying video programming that must not be shown or must be channeled to a later hour. For example, the definition used in a mandatory ratings regime intended to facilitate parental control might take into account a depiction's potential for harm without requiring a finding of a likelihood of harm. Ratings and blocking regulations might require multiple definitions for different kinds of violent programming to which parents might want to restrict their children's access. Another variable is what type and degree of violent content the research demonstrates, with a reasonable probability, is harmful to children.

40.   In addition, any definition would have to be sufficiently clear to provide fair

notice to regulated entities.   NAB and other commenters principally argue that violent programming cannot be sufficiently defined to give affected parties the requisite notice to be able to predictably comply with any such regulation. . . .

41.   Judicial decisions and scholarly articles discussing violence almost invariably make this definitional point by referencing classic works of literature of undisputed merit that involve graphic violence. For example, in a case involving violent video games, Judge Posner opined that even the sponsors of the regulation would no doubt concede that restrictions would not be warranted:

> if the question were whether to forbid children to read without the presence of an adult the Odyssey, with its graphic descriptions of Odysseus's grinding out the eye of Polyphemus with a heated, sharpened stake, killing the suitors, and hanging the treacherous maidservants; or The Divine Comedy with its graphic descriptions of the tortures of the damned; or War and Peace with its graphic descriptions of execution by firing squad, death in childbirth, and death from war wounds.

The UCLA Center for Communications Policy notes in its *1997 TV Violence Report*:

> For centuries, violence has been an important element of storytelling, and violent themes have been found in the Bible, The Iliad and The Odyssey, fairy tales, theater, literature, film and, of course, television. Descriptions of violence in the Bible have been important for teaching lessons and establishing a moral code. Lessons of the evils of jealousy and revenge are learned from the story of Cain and Abel. Early fairy tales were filled with violence and gruesomeness designed to frighten children into behaving and to teach them right from wrong.

42.   Several commenters advocate adopting specific definitions. Those that do chose pre-existing definitions in the literature or selected regulatory proxies as a model. For example, Pappas Telecasting suggests that the Commission essentially adopt the definition used by the *National TV Violence Study*, which defined violence as "any overt depiction of a credible threat of physical force or the actual use of such force intended to physically harm an animate being or group of beings."   Morality in Media ("MIM") suggests enhancing the existing indecency definition by including references to violence. According to MIM, indecent speech should be defined as content that, in context, describes or depicts: "(1) sexual or excretory activities or organs or (2) outrageously offensive or outrageously disgusting violence or (3) severed or mutilated human bodies or body parts, in terms patently offensive as measured by contemporary community standards for the broadcast medium."   MIM defines violence as: "intense, rough or injurious use of physical force or treatment either recklessly or with an apparent intent to harm."

44.   We believe that developing an appropriate definition of excessively violent programming would be possible, but such language needs to be narrowly tailored and in conformance with judicial precedent. Any definition would need to be clear enough to provide fair warning of the conduct required. A definition sufficient to give notice of upcoming violent programming content to parents and potential viewers could make use of, or be a refinement of, existing voluntary rating system definitions or could make use of definitions used in the research community when studying the consequences of violent programming. For more restrictive time channeling rules, a definition based on the scientific literature discussed above, which recognizes the factors most important to determining the likely impact of violence on the child audience,

could be developed. For example, such a definition might cover depictions of physical force against an animate being that, in context, are patently offensive. In determining whether such depictions are patently offensive, the Government could consider among other factors the presence of weapons, whether the violence is extensive or graphic, and whether the violence is realistic.

V.   CONCLUSIONS AND RECOMMENDATIONS

45.   In response to the specific questions posed, we draw the following conclusions. First, with respect to the evidence of harm to children from viewing violent television content, there is strong evidence that exposure to violence in the media can increase aggressive behavior in children, at least in the short term.

46.   Second, although there are constitutional barriers to directly limiting or time channeling the distribution of violent television programming, the Supreme Court's *Pacifica* decision and other decisions relating to restrictions on the broadcast of indecent content provide possible parallels for regulating violent television content.   Third, while there are legal, evidentiary, analytical, and social science obstacles that need to be overcome in defining harmful violence, Congress likely has the ability and authority to craft a sustainable definition.

49.   In sum, Congress could implement a time channeling solution, as discussed above, and/or mandate some other form of consumer choice in obtaining video programming, such as the provision by MVPDs of video channels provided on family tiers or on an a la carte basis (e.g., channel blocking and reimbursement).

NOTES AND QUESTIONS

1.   Passing the Buck. In his statement, Commissioner Jonathan Adelstein suggested that the FCC "passe[d] the buck" by failing to adopt or recommend any specific regulatory program. Should the FCC have been more specific in adopting a particular recommendation? What would you recommend?

2.   "If It Bleeds, It Leads." America is, as Commissioner Adelstein put it, "hooked on violence." Moreover, as Adelstein noted, "the top ten highest rated broadcast programs consistently have programs with violent content leading the pack." Can violence be eradicated from TV programming? What about news programming? Is any regulatory program aimed at limiting TV violence bound to be overbroad in its application?

3.   Turning Off the TV. Is the "off" option a sufficient safeguard? What about other media—the Internet, video games, or even content on cell phones. Are regulatory programs aimed at protecting children likely to be necessary in those contexts, too?

Chapter 8: Intro to MVPD Marketplace

Insert after 483 n. 9—Video Franchising Reform:

The effort to facilitate entry into video markets by telephone companies hit full stride at the end of 2006. In addition to an increasing number of states, including major ones such as California, Texas, and New Jersey, passing legislation providing for statewide franchising, the FCC adopted an order aimed at easing the path of telephone companies into video programming markets. Set forth below is an excerpted version of the FCC's Order.

Implementation of Section 621(a)(1) of the Cable Communications Policy Act of 1984
FCC 06-180, 2007 WL 654264 (March 5, 2007)

I. INTRODUCTION

1. In this Report and Order ("*Order*"), we adopt rules and provide guidance to implement Section 621(a)(1) of the Communications Act of 1934, as amended (the "Communications Act"), which prohibits franchising authorities from unreasonably refusing to award competitive franchises for the provision of cable services. We find that the current operation of the local franchising process in many jurisdictions constitutes an unreasonable barrier to entry that impedes the achievement of the interrelated federal goals of enhanced cable competition and accelerated broadband deployment. We further find that Commission action to address this problem is both authorized and necessary. Accordingly, we adopt measures to address a variety of means by which local franchising authorities, i.e., county- or municipal-level franchising authorities ("LFAs"), are unreasonably refusing to award competitive franchises. We anticipate that the rules and guidance we adopt today will facilitate and expedite entry of new cable competitors into the market for the delivery of video programming [i.e., cable services], and accelerate broadband deployment consistent with our statutory responsibilities.

2. New competitors are entering markets for the delivery of services historically offered by monopolists: traditional phone companies are primed to enter the cable market, while traditional cable companies are competing in the telephony market. Ultimately, both types of companies are projected to offer customers a "triple play" of voice, high-speed Internet access, and video services over their respective networks. We believe this competition for delivery of bundled services will benefit consumers by driving down prices and improving the quality of service offerings. We are concerned, however, that traditional phone companies seeking to enter the video market face unreasonable regulatory obstacles, to the detriment of competition generally and cable subscribers in particular.

3. The Communications Act sets forth the basic rules concerning what franchising authorities may and may not do in evaluating applications for competitive franchises. Despite the parameters established by the Communications Act, however, operation of the franchising process has proven far more complex and time consuming than it should be, particularly with respect to facilities-based telecommunications and broadband providers that already have access to rights-of-way. New entrants have demonstrated that they are willing and able to upgrade their networks to provide video services, but the current operation of the franchising process at the local level unreasonably delays and, in some cases, derails these efforts due to LFAs' unreasonable demands on competitive applicants. These delays discourage investment in the fiber-based infrastructure necessary for the provision of advanced broadband services, because franchise applicants do not have the promise of revenues from video services to offset the costs of such deployment. Thus, the current operation of the franchising process often not only

contravenes the statutory imperative to foster competition in the multichannel video programming distribution ("MVPD") market, but also defeats the congressional goal of encouraging broadband deployment.

4.   In light of the problems with the current operation of the franchising process, we believe that it is now appropriate for the Commission to exercise its authority and take steps to prevent LFAs from unreasonably refusing to award competitive franchises. We have broad rulemaking authority to implement the provisions of the Communications Act, including Title VI generally and Section 621(a)(1) in particular. In addition, Section 706 of the Telecommunications Act of 1996 directs the Commission to encourage broadband deployment by removing barriers to infrastructure investment, and the U.S. Court of Appeals for the District of Columbia Circuit has held that the Commission may fashion its rules to fulfill the goals of Section 706.

5.   To eliminate the unreasonable barriers to entry into the cable market, and to encourage investment in broadband facilities, we: (1) find that an LFA's failure to issue a decision on a competitive application within the time frames specified herein constitutes an unreasonable refusal to award a competitive franchise within the meaning of Section 621(a)(1); (2) find that an LFA's refusal to grant a competitive franchise because of an applicant's unwillingness to agree to unreasonable build-out mandates constitutes an unreasonable refusal to award a competitive franchise within the meaning of Section 621(a)(1); (3) find that unless certain specified costs, fees, and other compensation required by LFAs are counted toward the statutory 5 percent cap on franchise fees, demanding them could result in an unreasonable refusal to award a competitive franchise; (4) find that it would be an unreasonable refusal to award a competitive franchise if the LFA denied an application based upon a new entrant's refusal to undertake certain obligations relating to public, educational, and government ("PEG") and institutional networks ("I-Nets") and (5) find that it is unreasonable under Section 621(a)(1) for an LFA to refuse to grant a franchise based on issues related to non-cable services or facilities. Furthermore, we preempt local laws, regulations, and requirements, including level-playing-field provisions, to the extent they permit LFAs to impose greater restrictions on market entry than the rules adopted herein. We also adopt a Further Notice of Proposed Rulemaking ("FNPRM") seeking comment on how our findings in this *Order* should affect existing franchisees. In addition, the FNPRM asks for comment on local consumer protection and customer service standards as applied to new entrants.

II.   BACKGROUND

6.   ***Section 621.*** Any new entrant seeking to offer "cable service" as a "cable operator" becomes subject to the requirements of Title VI. Section 621 of Title VI sets forth general cable franchise requirements. Subsection (b)(1) of Section 621 prohibits a cable operator from providing cable service in a particular area without first obtaining a cable franchise, and subsection (a)(1) grants to franchising authorities the power to award such franchises.

7.   The initial purpose of Section 621(a)(1), which was added to the Communications Act by the Cable Communications Policy Act of 1984 (the "1984 Cable Act"), was to delineate the role of LFAs in the franchising process. As originally enacted, Section 621(a)(1) simply stated that "[a] franchising authority may award, in accordance with the provisions of this title, 1 or more franchises within its jurisdiction." A few years later, however, the Commission prepared a report to Congress on the cable industry pursuant to the requirements of the 1984 Cable Act. In that Report, the Commission concluded that in order "[t]o encourage more robust competition in the local video marketplace, the Congress should . . . forbid local

franchising authorities from unreasonably denying a franchise to potential competitors who are ready and able to provide service."

8.   In response, Congress revised Section 621(a)(1) through the Cable Television Consumer Protection and Competition Act of 1992 (the "1992 Cable Act") to read as follows: "A franchising authority may award, in accordance with the provisions of this title, 1 or more franchises within its jurisdiction; except that a franchising authority may not grant an exclusive franchise and *may not unreasonably refuse to award an additional competitive franchise.*" In the Conference Report on the legislation, Congress found that competition in the cable industry was sorely lacking:

> For a variety of reasons, including local franchising requirements and the extraordinary expense of constructing more than one cable television system to serve a particular geographic area, most cable television subscribers have no opportunity to select between competing cable systems. Without the presence of another multichannel video programming distributor, a cable system faces no local competition. The result is undue market power for the cable operator as compared to that of consumers and video programmers.

To address this problem, Congress abridged local government authority over the franchising process to promote greater cable competition:

> Based on the evidence in the record taken as a whole, it is clear that there are benefits from competition between two cable systems. Thus, the Committee believes that local franchising authorities should be encouraged to award second franchises. Accordingly, [the 1992 Cable Act] as reported, prohibits local franchising authorities from unreasonably refusing to grant second franchises.

As revised, Section 621(a)(1) establishes a clear, federal-level limitation on the authority of LFAs in the franchising process in order to "promote the availability to the public of a diversity of views and information through cable television and other video distribution media," and to "rely on the marketplace, to the maximum extent feasible, to achieve that availability." Congress further recognized that increased competition in the video programming industry would curb excessive rate increases and enhance customer service, two areas in particular which Congress found had deteriorated because of the monopoly power of cable operators brought about, at least in part, by the local franchising process.

9.   In 1992, Congress also revised Section 621(a)(1) to provide that "[a]ny applicant whose application for a second franchise has been denied by a final decision of the franchising authority may appeal such final decision pursuant to the provisions of section 635." Section 635, in turn, states that "[a]ny cable operator adversely affected by any final determination made by a franchising authority under section 621(a)(1) . . . may commence an action within 120 days after receiving notice of such determination" in federal court or a state court of general jurisdiction. Congress did not, however, provide an explicit judicial remedy for other forms of unreasonable refusals to award competitive franchises, such as an LFA's refusal to act on a pending franchise application within a reasonable time period.

10. ***The Local Franchising NPRM.*** Notwithstanding the limitation imposed on LFAs by Section 621(a)(1), prior to commencement of this proceeding, the Commission had seen indications that the current operation of the franchising process still serves as an unreasonable barrier to entry for potential new cable entrants into the MVPD market. In November 2005, the Commission issued a Notice of Proposed Rulemaking ("*Local Franchising NPRM*") to determine whether LFAs are unreasonably refusing to award competitive franchises and thereby impeding achievement of the statute's goals of increasing competition in the delivery of video programming and accelerating broadband deployment.

11. The Commission sought comment on the current environment in which new cable entrants attempt to obtain competitive cable franchises. For example, the Commission requested input on the number of: (a) LFAs in the United States; (b) competitive franchise applications filed to date; and (c) ongoing franchise negotiations. To determine whether the current operation of the franchising process discourages competition and broadband deployment, the Commission also sought information regarding, among other things:

- how much time, on average, elapses between the date a franchise application is filed and the date an LFA acts on the application, and during that period, how much time is spent in active negotiations;

- whether to establish a maximum time frame for an LFA to act on an application for a competitive franchise;

- whether "level-playing-field" mandates, which impose on new entrants terms and conditions identical to those in the incumbent cable operator's franchise, constitute unreasonable barriers to entry;

- whether build-out requirements (*i.e.*, requirements that a franchisee deploy cable service to parts or all of the franchise area within a specified period of time) are creating unreasonable barriers to competitive entry;

- specific examples of any monetary or in-kind LFA demands unrelated to cable services that could be adversely affecting new entrants' ability to obtain franchises; and

- whether current procedures or requirements are appropriate for any cable operator, including incumbent cable operators.

12. In the *Local Franchising NPRM*, we tentatively concluded that Section 621(a)(1) empowers the Commission to adopt rules to ensure that the franchising process does not unduly interfere with the ability of potential competitors to provide video programming to consumers. Accordingly, the Commission sought comment on how it could best remedy any problems with the current franchising process.

14. ***The Franchising Process.*** The record in this proceeding demonstrates that the franchising process differs significantly from locality to locality. In most states, franchising is conducted at the local level, affording counties and municipalities broad discretion in deciding whether to grant a franchise. Some counties and municipalities have cable ordinances that govern the structure of negotiations, while others may proceed on an applicant-by-applicant basis. Where franchising negotiations are focused at the local level, some LFAs create formal or informal consortia to pool their resources and expedite competitive entry.

15.   To provide video services over a geographic area that encompasses more than one LFA, a prospective entrant must become familiar with all applicable regulations. This is a time-consuming and expensive process that has a chilling effect on competitors. Verizon estimates, for example, that it will need 2,500-3,000 franchises in order to provide video services throughout its service area. AT&T states that its Project Lightspeed deployment is projected to cover a geographic area that would encompass as many as 2,000 local franchise areas. BellSouth estimates that there are approximately 1,500 LFAs within its service area. Qwest's in-region territory covers a potential 5,389 LFAs. While other companies are also considering competitive entry, these estimates amply demonstrate the regulatory burden faced by competitors that seek to enter the market on a wide scale, a burden that is amplified when individual LFAs unreasonably refuse to grant competitive franchises.

16.   A few states and municipalities recently have recognized the need for reform and have established expedited franchising processes for new entrants. Although these processes also vary greatly and thus are of limited help to new cable providers seeking to quickly enter the marketplace on a regional basis, they do provide more uniformity in the franchising process on an intrastate basis. These state level reforms appear to offer promise in assisting new entrants to more quickly begin offering consumers a competitive choice among cable providers. In 2005, the Texas legislature designated the Texas Public Utility Commission ("PUC") as the franchising authority for state-issued franchises, and required the PUC to issue a franchise within 17 business days after receipt of a completed application from an eligible applicant. In 2006, Indiana, Kansas, South Carolina, New Jersey, North Carolina, and California also passed legislation to streamline the franchising process by providing for expedited, state level grants of franchises. Virginia, by contrast, did not establish statewide franchises but mandated uniform time frames for negotiations, public hearings, and ultimate franchise approval at the local level. In particular, a "certificated provider of telecommunications service" with existing authority to use public rights-of-way is authorized to provide video service within 75 days of filing a request to negotiate with each individual LFA. Similarly, Michigan recently enacted legislation that streamlines the franchise application process, establishes a 30-day timeframe within which an LFA must make a decision, and eliminates build-out requirements.

17.   In some states, however, franchise reform efforts launched in recent months have failed. For example, in Florida, bills that would have allowed competitive providers to enter the market with a permit from the Office of the Secretary of State, and contained no build-out or service delivery schedules, died in committee. In Louisiana, the Governor vetoed a bill that would have created a state franchise structure, provided for automatic grant of an application 45 days after filing, and contained no build-out requirements. In Maine, a bill that would have replaced municipal franchises with state franchises was withdrawn. Finally, a Missouri bill that would have given the Public Service Commission the authority to grant franchises and would have prohibited local franchising died in committee.

III.   DISCUSSION

18.   Based on the voluminous record in this proceeding, which includes comments filed by new entrants, incumbent cable operators, LFAs, consumer groups, and others, we conclude that the current operation of the franchising process can constitute an unreasonable barrier to entry for potential cable competitors, and thus justifies Commission action. We find that we have authority under Section 621(a)(1) to address this problem by establishing limits on LFAs' ability to delay, condition, or otherwise "unreasonably refuse to award" competitive franchises. We find that we also have the authority to consider the goals of Section 706 in addressing this problem under Section 621(a)(1). We believe that, absent Commission action,

deployment of competitive video services by new cable entrants will continue to be unreasonably delayed or, at worst, derailed. Accordingly, we adopt incremental measures directed to LFA-controlled franchising processes, as described in detail below. We anticipate that the rules and guidance we adopt today will facilitate and expedite entry of new cable competitors into the market for the delivery of multichannel video programming and thus encourage broadband deployment.

A.   The Current Operation of the Franchising Process Unreasonably Interferes With Competitive Entry

19.   Most communities in the United States lack cable competition, which would reduce cable rates and increase innovation and quality of service. Although LFAs adduced evidence that they have granted some competitive franchises, and competitors acknowledge that they have obtained some franchises, the record includes only a few hundred examples of competitive franchises, many of which were obtained after months of unnecessary delay. In the vast majority of communities, cable competition simply does not exist.

20.   The dearth of competition is due, at least in part, to the franchising process. The record demonstrates that the current operation of the franchising process unreasonably prevents or, at a minimum, unduly delays potential cable competitors from entering the MVPD market. Numerous commenters have adduced evidence that the current operation of the franchising process constitutes an unreasonable barrier to entry. Regulatory restrictions and conditions on entry shield incumbents from competition and are associated with various economic inefficiencies, such as reduced innovation and distorted consumer choices. We recognize that some LFAs have made reasonable efforts to facilitate competitive entry into the video programming market. We also recognize that recent state level reforms have the potential to streamline the process to a noteworthy degree. We find, though, that the current operation of the local franchising process often is a roadblock to achievement of the statutory goals of enhancing cable competition and broadband deployment.

21.   Commenters have identified six factors that stand in the way of competitive entry. They are: (1) unreasonable delays by LFAs in acting on franchise applications; (2) unreasonable build-out requirements imposed by LFAs; (3) LFA demands unrelated to the franchising process; (4) confusion concerning the meaning and scope of franchise fee obligations; (5) unreasonable LFA demands for PEG channel capacity and construction of I-Nets; and (6) level-playing-field requirements set by LFAs. We address each factor below.

24.   Delays in acting on franchise applications are especially onerous because franchise applications are rarely denied outright, which would enable applicants to seek judicial review under Section 635. Rather, negotiations are often drawn out over an extended period of time. As a result, the record shows that numerous new entrants have accepted franchise terms they considered unreasonable in order to avoid further delay. Others have filed lawsuits seeking a court order compelling the LFA to act, which entails additional delay, legal uncertainty, and great expense. Alternatively, some prospective entrants have walked away from unduly prolonged negotiations. Moreover, delays provide the incumbent cable operator the opportunity to launch targeted marketing campaigns before the competitor's rollout, thus undermining a competitor's prospects for success.

26.   Incumbent cable operators and LFAs state that new entrants could gain rapid entry if the new entrants simply agreed to the same terms applied to incumbent cable franchisees. However, this is not a reasonable expectation generally, given that the circumstances surrounding competitive entry are considerably different than those in existence at the time incumbent cable

operators obtained their franchises. Incumbent cable operators originally negotiated franchise agreements as a means of acquiring or maintaining a monopoly position. In most instances, imposing the incumbent cable operator's terms and conditions on a new entrant would make entry prohibitively costly because the entrant cannot assume that it will quickly—or ever—amass the same number or percentage of subscribers that the incumbent cable operator captured. The record demonstrates that requiring entry on the same terms as incumbent cable operators may thwart entry entirely or may threaten new entrants' chances of success once in the market.

31.   ***Impact of Build-Out Requirements.*** The record shows that build-out issues are one of the most contentious between LFAs and prospective new entrants, and that build-out requirements can greatly hinder the deployment of new video and broadband services. New and potential entrants commented extensively on the adverse impact of build-out requirements on their deployment plans. Large incumbent LECs, small and mid-sized incumbent LECs, competitive LECs and others view build-out requirements as the most significant obstacle to their plans to deploy competitive video and broadband services. Similarly, consumer groups and the U.S. Department of Justice, Antitrust Division, urge the Commission to address this aspect of the current franchising process in order to speed competitive entry.

32.   The record demonstrates that build-out requirements can substantially reduce competitive entry. Numerous commenters urge the Commission to prohibit LFAs from imposing any build-out requirements, and particularly universal build-out requirements. They argue that imposition of such mandates, rather than resulting in the increased service throughout the franchise area that LFAs desire, will cause potential new entrants to simply refrain from entering the market at all. They argue that even build-out provisions that do not require deployment throughout an entire franchise area may prevent a prospective new entrant from offering service.

36.   In many cases, build-out requirements also adversely affect consumer welfare. DOJ noted that imposing uneconomical build-out requirements results in less efficient competition and the potential for higher prices. Non-profit research organizations the Mercatus Center and the Phoenix Center argue that build-out requirements reduce consumer welfare. Each conclude that build-out requirements imposed on competitive cable entrants only benefit an incumbent cable operator. The Mercatus Center, citing data from the FCC and GAO indicating that customers with a choice of cable providers enjoy lower rates, argues that, to the extent that build-out requirements deter entry, they result in fewer customers having a choice of providers and a resulting reduction in rates. The Phoenix Center study contends that build-out requirements deter entry and conflict with federal, state, and local government goals of rapid broadband deployment. Another research organization, the American Consumer Institute (ACI), concluded that build-out requirements are inefficient: if a cable competitor initially serves only one neighborhood in a community, and a few consumers in this neighborhood benefit from the competition, total welfare in the community improves because no consumer was made worse and some consumers (those who can subscribe to the competitive service) were made better. In comparison, requirements that deter competitive entry may make some consumers (those who would have been able to subscribe to the competitive service) worse off. In many instances, placing build-out conditions on competitive entrants harms consumers and competition because it increases the cost of cable service. Qwest commented that, in those communities it has not entered due to build-out requirements, consumers have been deprived of the likely benefit of lower prices as the result of competition from a second cable provider. This claim is supported by the Commission's 2005 annual cable price survey, in which the Commission observed that average monthly cable rates varied markedly depending on the presence—and type—of MVPD competition in the local market. The greatest difference occurred where there was wireline

overbuild competition, where average monthly cable rates were 20.6 percent lower than the average for markets deemed noncompetitive.

40.   Based on the record as a whole, we find that build-out requirements imposed by LFAs can constitute unreasonable barriers to entry for competitive applicants.   Indeed, the record indicates that because potential competitive entrants to the cable market may not be able to economically justify build-out of an entire local franchising area immediately, these requirements can have the effect of granting *de facto* exclusive franchises, in direct contravention of Section 621(a)(1)'s prohibition of exclusive cable franchises.

43.   ***LFA Demands Unrelated to the Provision of Video Services.***   Many commenters recounted franchise negotiation experiences in which LFAs made unreasonable demands unrelated to the provision of video services. Verizon, for example, described several communities that made unreasonable requests, such as the purchase of street lights, wiring for all houses of worship, the installation of cell phone towers, cell phone subsidies for town employees, library parking at Verizon's facilities, connection of 220 traffic signals with fiber optics, and provision of free wireless broadband service in an area in which Verizon's subsidiary does not offer such service. In Maryland, some localities conditioned a franchise upon Verizon's agreement to make its data services subject to local customer service regulation. AT&T provided examples of impediments that Ameritech New Media faced when it entered the market, including a request for a new recreation center and pool. FTTH Council highlighted Grande Communications' experience in San Antonio, which required that Grande Communications make an up-front, $1 million franchise fee payment and fund a $50,000 scholarship with additional annual contributions of $7,200. The record demonstrates that LFA demands unrelated to cable service typically are not counted toward the statutory 5 percent cap on franchise fees, but rather imposed on franchisees in addition to assessed franchise fees. Based on this record evidence, we are convinced that LFA requests for unreasonable concessions are not isolated, and that these requests impose undue burdens upon potential cable providers.

44.   ***Assessment of Franchise Fees.***   The record establishes that unreasonable demands over franchise fee issues also contribute to delay in franchise negotiations at the local level and hinder competitive entry. Fee issues include not only which franchise-related costs imposed on providers should be included within the 5 percent statutory franchise fee cap established in Section 622(b), but also the proper calculation of franchise fees (*i.e.*, the revenue base from which the 5 percent is calculated).   In Virginia, municipalities have requested large "acceptance fees" upon grant of a franchise, in addition to franchise fees. Other LFAs have requested consultant and attorneys' fees. Several Pennsylvania localities have requested franchise fees based on cable and non-cable revenues. Some commenters assert that an obligation to provide anything of value, including PEG costs, should apply toward the franchise fee obligation.

46.   ***PEG and I-Net Requirements.***   Negotiations over PEG and I-Nets also contribute to delays in the franchising process. In response to the *Local Franchising NPRM*, we received numerous comments asking for clarification of what requirements LFAs reasonably may impose on franchisees to support PEG and I-Nets. We also received comments suggesting that some LFAs are making unreasonable demands regarding PEG and I-Net support as a condition of awarding competitive franchises. LFAs have demanded funding for PEG programming and facilities that exceeds their needs, and will not provide an accounting of where the money goes. For example, one municipality in Florida requested $6 million for PEG facilities, and a Massachusetts community requested 10 PEG channels, when the incumbent cable operator only provides two. Several commenters argued that it is unreasonable for an LFA to request a number

of PEG channels from a new entrant that is greater than the number of channels that the community is using at the time the new entrant submits its franchise application. The record indicates that LFAs also have made what commenters view as unreasonable institutional network requests, such as free cell phones for employees, fiber optic service for traffic signals, and redundant fiber networks for public buildings.

47. ***Level-Playing-Field Provisions.*** The record demonstrates that, in considering franchise applications, some LFAs are constrained by so-called "level-playing-field" provisions in local laws or incumbent cable operator franchise agreements. Such provisions typically impose upon new entrants terms and conditions that are neither "more favorable" nor "less burdensome" than those to which existing franchisees are subject. Some LFAs impose level-playing-field requirements on new entrants even without a statutory, regulatory, or contractual obligation to do so. Minnesota's process allows incumbent cable operators to be active in a competitor's negotiation, and incumbent cable operators have challenged franchise grants when those incumbent cable operators believed that the LFA did not follow correct procedure. According to BellSouth, the length of time for approval of its franchises was tied directly to level-playing-field constraints; absent such demands (in Georgia, for example), the company's applications were granted quickly. NATOA contends, however, that although level-playing-field provisions sometimes can complicate the franchising process, they do not present unreasonable barriers to entry. NATOA and LFAs argue that level-playing-field provisions serve important policy goals, such as ensuring a competitive environment and providing for an equitable distribution of services and obligations among all operators.

48. The record demonstrates that local level-playing-field mandates can impose unreasonable and unnecessary requirements on competitive applicants. As noted above, level-playing-field provisions enable incumbent cable operators to delay or prevent new entry by threatening to challenge any franchise that an LFA grants. Comcast asserts that MSOs are well within their rights to insist that their legal and contractual rights are honored in the grant of a subsequent franchise. The record demonstrates, however, that local level-playing-field requirements may require LFAs to impose obligations on new entrants that directly contravene Section 621(a)(1)'s prohibition on unreasonable refusals to award a competitive franchise. In most cases, incumbent cable operators entered into their franchise agreements in exchange for a monopoly over the provision of cable service. Build-out requirements and other terms and conditions that may have been sensible under those circumstances can be unreasonable when applied to competitive entrants. NATOA's argument that level-playing-field requirements always serve to ensure a competitive environment and provide for an equitable distribution of services and obligations ignores that incumbent and competitive operators are not on the same footing. LFAs do not afford competitive providers the monopoly power and privileges that incumbents received when they agreed to their franchises, something that investors recognize.

50. ***Benefits of Cable Competition.*** We further agree with new entrants that reform of the operation of the franchise process is necessary and appropriate to achieve increased video competition and broadband deployment. The record demonstrates that new cable competition reduces rates far more than competition from DBS. Specifically, the presence of a second cable operator in a market results in rates approximately 15 percent lower than in areas without competition—about $5 per month. The magnitude of the rate decreases caused by wireline cable competition is corroborated by the rates charged in Keller, Texas, where the price for Verizon's "Everything" package is 13 percent below that of the incumbent cable operator, and in Pinellas County, Florida, where Knology is the overbuilder and the incumbent cable operator's rates are $10-15 lower than in neighboring areas where it faces no competition.

51.   We also conclude that broadband deployment and video entry are "inextricably linked" and that, because the current operation of the franchising process often presents an unreasonable barrier to entry for the provision of video services, it necessarily hampers deployment of broadband services. The record demonstrates that broadband deployment is not profitable without the ability to compete with the bundled services that cable companies provide. As the Phoenix Center explains, "the more potential revenues that the network can generate in a household, the more likely it is the network will be built to that household." DOJ's comments underscore that additional video competition will likely speed deployment of advanced broadband services to consumers. Thus, although LFAs only oversee the provision of wireline-based video services, their regulatory actions can directly affect the provision of voice and data services, not just cable. We find reasonable AT&T's assertion that carriers will not invest billions of dollars in network upgrades unless they are confident that LFAs will grant permission to offer video services quickly and without unreasonable difficulty.

B.   The Commission Has Authority to Adopt Rules to Implement Section 621(a)(1)

53.   In the *Local Franchising NPRM*, the Commission tentatively concluded that it has the authority to adopt rules implementing Title VI of the Act, including Section 621(a)(1). The Commission sought comment on whether it has the authority to adopt rules or whether it is limited to providing guidance. Based on the record and governing legal principles, we affirm this tentative conclusion and find that the Commission has the authority to adopt rules to implement Title VI and, more specifically, Section 621(a)(1).

54.   Congress delegated to the Commission the task of administering the Communications Act. As the Supreme Court has explained, the Commission serves "as the 'single Government agency' with 'unified jurisdiction' and 'regulatory power over all forms of electrical communication, whether by telephone, telegraph, cable, or radio.'" To that end, "[t]he Act grants the Commission broad responsibility to forge a rapid and efficient communications system, and broad authority to implement that responsibility." Section 201(b) authorizes the Commission to "prescribe such rules and regulations as may be necessary in the public interest to carry out the provisions of this Act." "[T]he grant in §201(b) means what it says: The FCC has rulemaking authority to carry out the 'provisions of this Act.'" This grant of authority therefore necessarily includes Title VI of the Communications Act in general, and Section 621(a)(1) in particular. Other provisions in the Act reinforce the Commission's general rulemaking authority. Section 303(r), for example, states that "the Commission from time to time, as public convenience, interest, or necessity requires shall . . . make such rules and regulations and prescribe such restrictions and conditions, not inconsistent with law, as may be necessary to carry out the provisions of this Act . . . ." Section 4(i) states that the Commission "may perform any and all acts, make such rules and regulations, and issue such orders, not inconsistent with this Act, as may be necessary in the execution of its functions."

56.   Although several commenters disagreed with our tentative conclusion, none has persuaded us that the Commission lacks the authority to adopt rules to implement Section 621(a)(1). Incumbent cable operators and franchise authorities argue that the judicial review provisions in Sections 621(a)(1) and 635 indicate that Congress gave the courts exclusive jurisdiction to interpret and enforce Section 621(a)(1), including authority to decide what constitutes an unreasonable refusal to award a competitive cable franchise. We find, however, that this argument reads far too much into the judicial review provisions. The mere existence of a judicial review provision in the Communications Act does not, by itself, strip the Commission of its otherwise undeniable rulemaking authority. As a general matter, the fact that Congress

provides a mechanism for judicial review to remedy a violation of a statutory provision does not deprive an agency of the authority to issue rules interpreting that statutory provision. Here, nothing in the statutory language or the legislative history suggests that by providing a judicial remedy, Congress intended to divest the Commission of the authority to adopt and enforce rules implementing Section 621. In light of the Commission's broad rulemaking authority under Section 201 and other provisions in the Act, the absence of a specific grant of rulemaking authority in Section 621 is "not peculiar." Other provisions in the Act demonstrate that when Congress intended to grant exclusive jurisdiction, it said so in the legislation. Here, however, neither Section 621(a)(1) nor Section 635 includes an exclusivity provision, and we decline to read one into either provision.

58.   We also reject the argument by some incumbent cable operators and franchise authorities that Section 621(a)(1) is unambiguous and contains no gaps in the statutory language that would give the Commission authority to regulate the franchising process. We strongly disagree. Congress did not define the term "unreasonably refuse," and it is far from self-explanatory. The United States Court of Appeals for the District of Columbia Circuit has held that the term "unreasonable" is among the "ambiguous statutory terms" in the Communications Act, and that the "court owes substantial deference to the interpretation the Commission accords them." We therefore find that Section 621(a)(1)'s requirement that an LFA "may not unreasonably refuse to award an additional competitive franchise" creates ambiguity that the Commission has the authority to resolve. The possibility that a court, in reviewing a particular matter, may determine whether an LFA "unreasonably" denied a second franchise does not displace the Commission's authority to adopt rules generally interpreting what constitutes an "unreasonable refusal" under Section 621(a)(1).

59.   Some incumbent cable operators and franchise authorities argue that Section 621(a)(1) imposes no general duty of reasonableness on the LFA in connection with procedures for *awarding* a competitive franchise. According to these commenters, the "unreasonably refuse to award" language in the first sentence in Section 621(a)(1) must be read in conjunction with the second sentence, which relates to the *denial* of a competitive franchise application. Based on this, commenters claim that "unreasonably refuse to award" means "unreasonably *deny*" and, thus, Section 621(a)(1) is not applicable before a final decision is rendered. We disagree. By concluding that the language "unreasonably refuse to award" means the same thing as "unreasonably deny," commenters violate the long-settled principle of statutory construction that each word in a statutory scheme must be given meaning. We find that the better reading of the phrase "unreasonably refuse to award" is that Congress intended to cover LFA conduct beyond ultimate denials by final decision, such as situations where an LFA has unreasonably refused to award an additional franchise by withholding a final decision or by insisting on unreasonable terms that an applicant refuses to accept. While the judicial review provisions in Sections 621(a)(1) and 635 refer to a "final decision" or "final determination," the Commission's rulemaking authority under Section 621 is not constrained in the same manner. Instead, the Commission has the authority to address what constitutes an unreasonable refusal to award a franchise, and as stated above, a local franchising authority may unreasonably refuse to award a franchise through other routes than issuing a final decision or determination denying a franchise application. For all of these reasons, we conclude that the Commission may exercise its statutory authority to establish federal standards identifying those LFA-imposed terms and conditions that would violate Section 621(a)(1) of the Communications Act.

60.   Incumbent cable operators and local franchise authorities also maintain that the legislative history of Section 621(a)(1) demonstrates that Congress reserved to LFAs the authority to determine what constitutes "reasonable" grounds for franchise denials, with oversight by the

courts, and left no authority under Section 621(a)(1) for the Commission to issue rules or guidelines governing the franchise approval process. Commenters point to the Conference Committee Report on the 1992 Amendments, which adopted the Senate version of Section 621, rather than the House version, which "contained five examples of circumstances under which it is reasonable for a franchising authority to deny a franchise." We find commenters' reliance on the legislative history to be misplaced. While the House may have initially considered adopting a categorical approach for determining what would constitute a "reasonable *denial*," Congress ultimately decided to forgo that approach and prohibit franchising authorities from unreasonably refusing to *award* an additional competitive franchise. To be sure, commenters are correct to point out that Congress chose not to define in the Act the meaning of the phrase "unreasonably refuse to award." However, commenters' assertion that Congress therefore intended for this gap in the statute to be filled in by only LFAs and courts lacks any basis in law or logic. Rather, we believe that it is far more reasonable to assume, consistent with settled principles of administrative law, that Congress intended that the Commission, which is charged by Congress with the administration of Title VI, to have the authority to do so. There is nothing in the statute or the legislative history to suggest that Congress intended to displace the Commission's explicit authority to interpret and enforce provisions in Title VI, including Section 621(a)(1).

64.   In sum, we conclude that we have clear authority to interpret and implement the Cable Act, including the ambiguous phrase "unreasonably refuse to award" in Section 621(a)(1), to further the congressional imperatives to promote competition and broadband deployment. As discussed above, this authority is reinforced by Section 4(i) of the Communications Act, which gives us broad power to perform acts necessary to execute our functions, and the mandate in Section 706 of the Telecommunications Act of 1996 that we encourage broadband deployment through measures that promote competition. We adopt the rules and regulations in this *Order* pursuant to that authority. We find that Section 621(a)(1) prohibits not only an LFA's ultimate unreasonable denial of a competitive franchise application, but also LFA procedures and conduct that have the effect of unreasonably interfering with the ability of a would-be competitor to obtain a competitive franchise, whether by (1) creating unreasonable delays in the process, or (2) imposing unreasonable regulatory roadblocks, such that they effectively constitute an "unreasonable refusal to award an additional competitive franchise" within the meaning of Section 621(a)(1).

C.   Steps to Ensure that the Local Franchising Process Does Not Unreasonably Interfere with Competitive Cable Entry and Rapid Broadband Deployment

65.   Commenters in this proceeding identified several specific issues regarding problems with the current operation of the franchising process. These include: (1) failure by LFAs to grant or deny franchises within reasonable time frames; (2) LFA requirements that a facilities-based new entrant build out its cable facilities beyond a reasonable service area; (3) certain LFA-mandated costs, fees, and other compensation and whether they must be counted toward the statutory 5 percent cap on franchise fees; (4) new entrants' obligations to provide support mandated by LFAs for PEG and I-Nets; and (5) facilities-based new entrants' obligations to comply with local consumer protection and customer service standards when the same facilities are used to provide other regulated services, such as telephony. . . .

71.   Based on our examination of the record, we believe that a time limit of 90 days for those applicants that have access to rights-of-way strikes the appropriate balance between the goals of facilitating competitive entry into the video marketplace and ensuring that franchising authorities have sufficient time to fulfill their responsibilities. In this vein, we note that 90 days is a considerably longer time frame than that suggested by some commenters, such as TIA. Additionally, we recognize that the Communications Act gives an LFA 120 days to make a final

decision on a cable operator's request to modify a franchise. We believe that the record supports an even shorter time here because the costs associated with delay are much greater with respect to entry. When an incumbent cable franchisee requests a modification, consumers are not deprived of service while an LFA deliberates. Here, delay by an individual LFA deprives consumers of the benefits of cable competition. An LFA should be able to negotiate a franchise with a familiar applicant that is already authorized to occupy the right-of-way in less than 120 days. The list of legitimate issues to be negotiated is short, and we narrow those issues considerably in this *Order*. We therefore impose a deadline of 90 days for an LFA to reach a final decision on a competitive franchise application submitted by those applicants authorized to occupy rights-of-way within the franchise area.

72.   For other applicants, we believe that six months affords a reasonable amount of time to negotiate with an entity that is not already authorized to occupy the right-of-way, as an LFA will need to evaluate the entity's legal, financial, and technical capabilities in addition to generally considering the applicant's fitness to be a communications provider over the rights-of-way. Commenters have presented substantial evidence that six months provides LFAs sufficient time to review an applicant's proposal, negotiate acceptable terms, and award or deny a competitive franchise. We are persuaded by the record that a six-month period will allow sufficient time for review. Given that LFAs must act on modification applications within the 120-day limit set by the Communications Act, we believe affording an additional two months—*i.e.*, a six-month review period—will provide LFAs ample time to conduct negotiations with an entity new to the franchise area.

73.   Failure of an LFA to act within these time frames is unreasonable and constitutes a refusal to award a competitive franchise. Consistent with other time limits that the Communications Act and our rules impose, a franchising authority and a competitive applicant may extend these limits if both parties agree to an extension of time. We further note that an LFA may engage in franchise review activities that are not prohibited by the Communications Act or our rules, such as multiple levels of review or holding a public hearing, provided that a final decision is made within the time period established under this *Order*.

77.   In the event that an LFA fails to grant or deny an application by the deadline set by the Commission, Verizon urges the Commission to temporarily authorize the applicant to provide video service. In general, we agree with this proposed remedy. In order to encourage franchising authorities to reach a final decision on a competitive application within the applicable time frame set forth in this *Order*, a failure to abide by the Commission's deadline must bring with it meaningful consequences. Additionally, we do not believe that a sufficient remedy for an LFA's inaction on an application is the creation of a remedial process, such as arbitration, that will result in even further delay. . . . Therefore, if an LFA has not made a final decision within the time limits we adopt in this *Order*, the LFA will be deemed to have granted the applicant an interim franchise based on the terms proposed in the application. This interim franchise will remain in effect only until the LFA takes final action on the application. We believe this approach is preferable to having the Commission itself provide interim franchises to applicants because a "deemed grant" will begin the process of developing a working relationship between the competitive applicant and the franchising authority, which will be helpful in the event that a negotiated franchise is ultimately approved.

2.   Build-Out

82.   As discussed above, build-out requirements in many cases may constitute unreasonable barriers to entry into the MVPD market for facilities-based competitors.

Accordingly, we limit LFAs' ability to impose certain build-out requirements pursuant to Section 621(a)(1).

a. Authority

83.   Proponents of build-out requirements do not offer any persuasive legal argument that the Commission lacks authority to address this significant problem and conclude that certain build-out requirements for competitive entrants are unreasonable.   Nothing in the Communications Act requires competitive franchise applicants to agree to build-out their networks in any particular fashion.   Nevertheless, incumbent cable operators and LFAs contend that it is both lawful and appropriate, in all circumstances, to impose the same build-out requirements on competitive applicants that apply to incumbents.   We reject these arguments and find that Section 621(a)(1) prohibits LFAs from refusing to award a new franchise on the ground that the applicant will not agree to unreasonable build-out requirements.

b. Discussion

87.   Given the current state of the MVPD marketplace, we find that an LFA's refusal to award a competitive franchise because the applicant will not agree to specified build-out requirements can be unreasonable.   Market conditions today are far different from when incumbent cable operators obtained their franchises.   Incumbent cable providers were frequently awarded community-wide monopolies.   In that context, a requirement that the provider build out facilities to the entire community was eminently sensible.   The essential bargain was that the cable operator would provide service to an entire community in exchange for its status as the only franchisee from whom customers in the community could purchase service.   Thus, a financial burden was placed upon the monopoly provider in exchange for the undeniable benefit of being able to operate without competition.

* * *

122.   We further clarify that an LFA may not use its video franchising authority to attempt to regulate a LEC's entire network beyond the provision of cable services.   We agree with Verizon that the "entirety of a telecommunications/data network is not automatically converted to a 'cable system' once subscribers start receiving video programming."   For instance, we find that the provision of video services pursuant to a cable franchise does not provide a basis for customer service regulation by local law or franchise agreement of a cable operator's entire network, or any services beyond cable services.   Local regulations that attempt to regulate any non-cable services offered by video providers are preempted because such regulation is beyond the scope of local franchising authority and is inconsistent with the definition of "cable system" in Section 602(7)(C).   This provision explicitly states that a common carrier facility subject to Title II is considered a cable system "to the extent such facility is used in the transmission of video programming . . . ."   As discussed above, revenues from non-cable services are not included in the base for calculation of franchise fees.

D. Preemption of Local Laws, Regulations and Requirements

125.   Having established rules and guidance to implement Section 621(a)(1), we turn now to the question of local laws that may be inconsistent with our decision today.   Because the rules we adopt represent a reasonable interpretation of relevant provisions in Title VI as well as a reasonable accommodation of the various policy interests that Congress entrusted to the Commission, they have preemptive effect pursuant to Section 636(c).   Alternatively, local laws are impliedly preempted to the extent that they conflict with this *Order* or stand as an obstacle to

the accomplishment and execution of the full purposes and objectives of Congress.

126.   At that outset of this discussion, it is important to reiterate that we do not preempt state law or state level franchising decisions in this *Order*. Instead, we preempt only local laws, regulations, practices, and requirements to the extent that: (1) provisions in those laws, regulations, practices, and agreements conflict with the rules or guidance adopted in this *Order*; and (2) such provisions are not specifically authorized by state law. As noted above, we conclude that the record before us does not provide sufficient information to make determinations with respect to franchising decisions where a state is involved, issuing franchises at the state level or enacting laws governing specific aspects of the franchising process. We expressly limit our findings and regulations in this *Order* to actions or inactions at the local level where a state has not circumscribed the LFA's authority. For example, in light of differences between the scope of franchises issued at the state level and those issued at the local level, it may be necessary to use different criteria for determining what may be unreasonable with respect to the key franchising issues addressed herein. We also recognize that many states only recently have enacted comprehensive franchise reform laws designed to facilitate competitive entry. In light of these facts, we lack a sufficient record to evaluate whether and how such state laws may lead to unreasonable refusals to award additional competitive franchises.

131.   We reject the claim by incumbent cable operators and franchising authorities that the Commission lacks authority to preempt local requirements because Congress has not explicitly granted the Commission the authority to preempt. These commenters suggest that because the Commission seeks to preempt a power traditionally exercised by a state or local government (*i.e.*, local franchising), under the Fifth Circuit's decision in *City of Dallas*, the Commission can only preempt where it is given express statutory authority to do so. However, this argument ignores the plain language of Section 636(c), which states that "any provision of law of any State, political subdivision, or agency therefore, or franchising authority . . . which is inconsistent with this chapter shall be deemed to be preempted and superseded." Moreover, Section 621 expressly limits the authority of franchising authorities by prohibiting exclusive franchises and unreasonable refusals to award additional competitive franchises. Congress could not have stated its intent to limit local franchising authority more clearly. These provisions therefore satisfy any express preemption requirement.

136.   Finally, LFAs maintain that the Commission's preemption of local governmental powers offends the Tenth Amendment of the U.S. Constitution. The Tenth Amendment provides that "[t]he powers not delegated to the United States by the Constitution, nor prohibited by it to the States, are reserved to the States respectively, or to the people." In support of their position, commenters argue that the Commission is improperly attempting to override local government's duty to "maximize the value of local property for the greater good" by imposing a federal regulatory scheme onto the states and/or local governments. Contrary to the local franchising authorities' claim, however, they have failed to demonstrate any violation of the Tenth Amendment. "If a power is delegated to Congress in the Constitution, the Tenth Amendment expressly disclaims any reservation of that power to the States." Thus, when Congress acts within the scope of its authority under the Commerce Clause, no Tenth Amendment issue arises. Regulation of cable services is well within Congress' authority under the Commerce Clause. Thus, because our authority in this area derives from a proper exercise of congressional power, the Tenth Amendment poses no obstacle to our preemption of state and local franchise law or practices. Likewise, there is no merit to LFA commenters' suggestion that Commission regulation of the franchising process would constitute an improper "commandeering" of state governmental power. The Supreme Court has recognized that "where Congress has the authority to regulate private activity under the Commerce Clause," Congress has the "power to offer States

the choice of regulating that activity according to federal standards or having state law preempted by federal regulation." And here, we are simply requiring local franchising authorities to exercise their regulatory authority according to federal standards, or else local requirements will be preempted. For all of these reasons, our actions today do not offend the Tenth Amendment.

NOTES AND QUESTIONS

1.   **Competition Versus Rate Regulation.** Until the Telecommunications Act of 1996 rejected the concept of rate regulation of cable services, regulation represented the primary strategy for protecting consumers against monopoly pricing. But Congress concluded that satellite TV firms, which had already begun to emerge as competitors to cable operators, as well as telephone companies would protect consumers by offering a choice in the marketplace. Satellite TV firms did, in fact, pick up considerable market share, but telephone companies largely stayed on the sidelines. Over the decade between 1995 to 2005, according to the Commission, cable rates rose 93% while other telecommunications services declined in price. Does that mean that competition has failed, that competition takes time, or that the statistics (which do not focus on improvements in the quantity or quality of cable programming) are flawed?

2.   **Section 621.** When written and over the decade that followed, this section largely governed the denial of a franchise to a second entrant. In 2005, however, the Commission commenced a rulemaking that gave rise to the Order excerpted above. Should the Commission enjoy authority to imbue new meaning into legislative language? Is the passage of time relevant to that authority? Note that Commissioner Adelstein dissented from the Order, explaining that the Commission cannot act when it "does not really define specific statutory terms, but rather takes off from those terms and devises a comprehensive regulatory regimen."

3.   **Build-Out Requirements.** One of the most controversial issues related to local franchises to second entrants is whether a requirement to build out service to all consumers is a legitimate requirement. To those entrants, such a requirement presents a formidable barrier to entry. To the cable incumbents, such a burden is framed as a "level playing field requirement." What is the right policy on build-out requirements?

4.   **Federalism and Localism.** To Commissioner Adelstein, the decision was "a clear rebuke of this storied relationship with local government . . . [and] a one-size-fits-all approach is antithetical to clear congressional intent that cable systems be 'responsive to needs and interests of local community.'" But if the federal government can embrace a pro-consumer solution, should it hesitate to do so? Does it matter that the decision displaced local authority, but not state authority? What justifies such a distinction?

5.   **Congressional Action Versus Agency Action.** Does it matter that Congress, at the time of the FCC's decision, had been considering franchising reform legislation? Why or why not?

6.   **The Shot Clock.** A central part of the Commission's order is a 90-day shot clock. Is it reasonable to believe that delays in negotiation are caused by the municipality and not the applicant? How can this regime ensure a requirement to negotiate in good faith?

Chapter 9:   Content

Insert after 567 n. 5:

The ongoing saga over how the must-carry rules will apply after the digital transition continues as the February, 2009 transition date approaches. In the spring of 2006, FCC Chairman Martin failed to garner sufficient support for his proposal that the broadcasters receive a must-carry right for all of the programs that they transmit using their digital TV systems. (A digital broadcast system can transmit six channels equivalent to traditional analog quality or one channel in high definition.) In April of 2007, Chairman Martin offered an alternative proposal set out in a Notice of Proposed Rulemaking—that cable providers must carry an analog signal of all broadcast programming to their customers who do not subscribe to digital cable service. This proposal is significant because, as of early 2007, more than half of cable customers did not subscribe to a digital package (which requires a set-top box) and thus would not necessarily have access to broadcast programming if the must-carry requirement applied only to digital programming.

Chairman Martin's proposal relies on his interpretation of the 1992 Cable Act's must-carry provision as requiring that cable operators ensure that every cable customer has a legal right to view all broadcast stations. As a practical matter, this interpretation, if adopted, would require cable systems to carry both digital and analog signals until every cable subscriber subscribed to a digital service. The cable industry, which has suggested that it would ensure that their customers could view all broadcast programming and has reached a number of agreements to do so, objected to the FCC's action. A cable spokesman responded to the Commission's announcement by stating that "[t]he FCC's current proposal appears to mandate an unnecessary and unconstitutional carriage requirement that has already been overwhelmingly rejected twice by the FCC." Ted Hearn, FCC Tees Up Dual Carriage Plan, Multichannel News (April 18, 2007) (http://www.multichannel.com/article/CA6434962.html).

Chapter 11:   Emerging Issues in Video Marketplace

Insert after 653 n. 7:

The FCC's role in overseeing digital copyright issues ended with the D.C. Circuit's decision in the Broadcast Flag matter. The rise of new video technologies, ranging from digital video recorders to Internet-based video programming available on YouTube, continues, however, to create numerous legal issues. In some cases, the issues test traditional copyright doctrines—such as the "fair use" doctrine (see the *Grokster* case reprinted at 948)—and other cases test more recent laws, such as the Digital Millennium Copyright Act (DMCA), which protects service providers that host content on the Internet. Two exemplary disputes that heated up in 2007 were a challenge to Cablevision's use of a server-based DVR and a challenge by Viacom to YouTube's claim that the DMCA shielded it from liability for the posting of copyrighted videos (provided that those videos were taken down when requested).

In March, 2007, Viacom filed an action against YouTube, requesting over $1 billion on the ground that the website (owned by Google) failed to prevent the posting of copyrighted content. Viacom's General Counsel, Mike Fricklas, rejected YouTube's defense that its status as an interactive service video immunized it from liability under the DMCA—"[t]hese [DMCA] provisions were tailored for AOL and their like because these services couldn't know everything that was going on in their chat rooms. YouTube is a different business." By contrast, Alexander Macgillivray, a Google associate general counsel, countered that the DMCA is "a relatively clear statute, and Web hosts in general have been confident their activity is not something that will subject them to copyright liability as long as they comply with the notice and takedown procedures outlined in the act."

Not long after Viacom filed its action against YouTube, the Southern District of New York ruled that Cablevision's server-based digital video recorder violated the Copyright Act. An excerpted version of this decision is set forth below.

TWENTIETH CENTURY FOX FILM CORP. V. CABLEVISION SYSTEMS CORP.
478 F.Supp.2d 607 (S.D.N.Y. 2007)

CHIN, District Judge.

In March 2006, Cablevision Systems Corporation ("Cablevision") announced that it would be rolling out a "new Remote-Storage DVR System" (the "RS-DVR"). The RS-DVR is intended for Cablevision customers who do not have a digital video recorder ("DVR") in their homes. The RS-DVR would permit these customers to record programs on central servers at Cablevision's facilities and play the programs back for viewing at home.

Cablevision has not obtained permission from plaintiffs, the owners of the copyrighted programs, to reproduce and transmit the programs through its proposed RS-DVR. It contends that a license is not required because the customer, not Cablevision, chooses the content and records the programs for personal viewing. It argues that, under *Sony Corp. v. Universal City Studios, Inc.,* 464 U.S. 417 (1984) a company cannot be liable for infringement merely because it supplies Betamax recorders, video cassette recorders ("VCRs"), or DVRs to consumers to record television programs for in-home, personal viewing, and it further contends that its RS-DVR is no different from these traditional devices.

In these related cases, plaintiffs sue Cablevision and its parent, CSC Holdings, Inc. ("CSC"), for copyright infringement, seeking a declaratory judgment that Cablevision's RS-DVR would violate their copyrights and an injunction enjoining defendants from rolling out the RS-DVR without copyright licenses. Defendants counterclaim for a declaratory judgment holding that the RS-DVR would not infringe on plaintiffs' copyrights. The parties' cross-motions for summary judgment are before the Court.

Plaintiffs' motions are granted and defendants' motion is denied, for I conclude that Cablevision, and not just its customers, would be engaging in unauthorized reproductions and transmissions of plaintiffs' copyrighted programs under the RS-DVR. Indeed, the RS-DVR is not a stand-alone machine that sits on top of a television. Rather, it is a complex system that involves an ongoing relationship between Cablevision and its customers, payment of monthly fees by the customers to Cablevision, ownership of the equipment remaining with Cablevision, the use of numerous computers and other equipment located in Cablevision's private facilities, and the ongoing maintenance of the system by Cablevision personnel. Accordingly, judgment will be entered in favor of plaintiffs.

STATEMENT OF THE CASE

Traditionally, television signals were transmitted in analog form. In other words, the signals were transmitted as a series of continuous waves. Today, television signals are increasingly delivered in digital form. Digital signals are transmitted as compressed data in the form of binary digits, or "bits." The number of bits that can be sent in a second is known as the "bitrate." Digital signals allow for a greater variety in television programming-because more signals can be transmitted in the same space-as well as interactive services and, often, better audio and image quality than analog television. The RS-DVR would be offered as part of Cablevision's digital cable service.

Digital cable delivery starts with programming owners sending feeds of their content to the cable company, which collects the feeds at a "head-end," a central facility that houses much of the software and hardware necessary to operate a cable system. For linear channels, the cable company collects all of the feeds into an "aggregated programming stream" ("APS"). The APS is composed of packets of data, each 188 bytes in size. Each packet is tagged with a "program identifier" ("PID") indicating the program to which it belongs.

The APS is sent from the head-end to customers' homes through a process known as Quadrature Amplitude Modulation ("QAM"); the devices used to accomplish this process are called QAM modulators. QAM converts the digital signals into radio frequency ("RF") signals, which are more robust and better suited for transmission along a cable system's coaxial cable lines. The RF signals are sent over the coaxial network (the "RF Distribution Network"), which routes the signals to the various "nodes" or service groups-smaller cable systems connecting a group of homes-comprising the cable system. Each node is serviced by a particular QAM modulator. The RF signals are typically then routed to the customer's digital set-top box. The packets of the APS are filtered according to their PIDs and reassembled into a single program transport stream to be decrypted, decoded, and displayed. To limit access to certain programming such as premium channels, the cable company encrypts the packets in the APS. The set-top box has decryption hardware that "unlocks" the encrypted packets.

ii. *Video-on-Demand*

Cable companies also provide certain services on an individual customer basis. Video-on-Demand ("VOD") is one such service. VOD allows a customer, using an on-screen menu and the remote control, to view at any time programming selected by the cable company. Pursuant to licenses negotiated with the programming owners, the cable company receives programming for VOD exhibition at its head-end, where the content is stored on computers. The cable company delivers the VOD content on extra channel frequencies that are not being used for linear programming.

VOD also requires a "reverse" channel for each customer, so that the customer can communicate with the cable company to select the desired programming and control the playback (i.e. rewind, fast-forward, and pause). These playback control functions are known as "trick modes." Cablevision offers VOD to its digital cable customers, pursuant to licensing agreements it has with the programming owners.

3. *Recording Television Programming: VCRs and DVRs*

VCRs, introduced for home use more than 25 years ago, provided the first practical means for television viewers to record programming. VCRs capture programming from television signals and record it onto magnetic tape housed in a video cassette. DVRs were introduced to consumers in 1999 and are increasingly being used in place of VCRs to record television programming. DVRs record programming to a hard-drive based digital storage medium, rather than to a video cassette.

Many cable companies offer "set-top storage DVRs" ("STS-DVRs"), which combine the function of a standard cable set-top box and a DVR. An STS-DVR can record digital programming streams directly (*i.e.,* without decoding them) onto a hard drive contained within the box. It may incorporate two tuners, allowing the customer to watch live programming on one channel and record on another, or record two channels simultaneously. Customers with STS-DVRs use an on-screen program guide to select the programs they wish to record. Once recorded, programming is stored on the box's hard drive and is available for playback. The customer can use certain trick modes to control playback. The amount of programming that can be stored depends on the size of the box's hard drive.

Cablevision has offered Cablevision-owned STS-DVRs to its digital cable customers, for an additional fee, since November 2004. A program may be recorded only if it is included within the tier of linear programming for which the customer has paid (the customer's "subscription programming"). Customers cannot, for example, use the STS-DVR to record pay-per-view or VOD programming.

4. *Cablevision's RS-DVR*

The RS-DVR is a type of network DVR ("nDVR"). An nDVR stores recorded programming in a central cable facility, rather than on the hard disk of the set-top box in the customer's home. The RS-DVR would store recorded programming remotely on computer servers located at Cablevision head-ends. The RS-DVR uses various components, including: (1) a remote control-the same one offered with Cablevision's STS-DVRs; (2) an on-screen program guide populated by data stored in a server located at the head-end-the same interface used by Cablevision's other digital cable customers; (3) a set-top box located in the customer's home; (4) "a network of wires, relays, switches, and RF devices connecting the set-top box . . . to Cablevision's cable television system"; and (5) computer hardware and software located at Cablevision's head-ends. Cablevision would charge its customers an additional fee for their use of the RS-DVR.

Recorded programming would be stored on servers designed by Arroyo Video Solutions, Inc. (each, an "Arroyo server") containing multiple hard disk drives. Each customer would be allotted a specified amount of storage capacity on one of those hard drives; his or her recorded programming would be stored in that hard drive space and available only to that customer. Cablevision determines the amount of memory allotted to each customer; initially, Cablevision contemplated allocating 80 megabytes of memory to each customer, but later decided on 160 megabytes. A recorded program would be stored indefinitely on the Arroyo server until selected for deletion by the customer or automatically overwritten by Cablevision on a first-in, first-out basis to make room for another program.

As the above description makes clear, the RS-DVR is not a single piece of equipment. Rather, it is a complex system requiring numerous computers, processes, networks of cables, and facilities staffed by personnel twenty-four hours a day and seven days a week. Cablevision's expert estimated that some ten "boxes" would be involved for each Arroyo server. Plaintiffs' expert testified that the RS-DVR "service"-or at least some of it-was housed in a "big room" at Cablevision's facilities, approximately 60 feet by 60 feet. Moreover, in general a Cablevision RS-DVR customer would not be able to walk into Cablevision's facilities and touch the RS-DVR system.

* * *

An RS-DVR customer can request that a program be recorded from any linear channel within his or her subscription programming in one of two ways. First, the customer can use the remote control to navigate the on-screen program guide and schedule a future program to record. The customer scrolls through a list of channels and programs, then presses the "record" button. Second, while watching a program, the customer can simply press "record" on the remote control.

When the set-top box receives the record command from the remote control, it relays the command to the "Application Data Server" ("ADS") server located at the head-end. The ADS verifies that: (1) the customer is authorized to receive the program in question; (2) the customer has not already requested that the program be recorded; (3) the customer has available hard drive storage space; (4) the recording of the program will not result in the customer's recording more than two programs at the same time; and (5) the customer is not trying to record a program that is not within his or her subscription programming. If any of the above criteria are not met, the RS-DVR causes an error message to be displayed on the customer's television screen with the appropriate remedial steps for the customer to take.

* * *

B. *Copyright Infringement*

The Copyright Act of 1976 (the "Copyright Act"), 17 U.S.C. §101 *et seq.,* confers upon copyright owners the exclusive rights to, among other things, "reproduce the copyrighted work in copies" and "in the case of . . . audiovisual works, to perform the copyrighted work publicly." *Id.* §§106(1) and (4) (2002). "To establish a claim of copyright infringement, a plaintiff must establish (1) ownership of a valid copyright and (2) unauthorized copying or a violation of one of the other exclusive rights afforded copyright owners pursuant to the Copyright Act."

Here, it is undisputed that plaintiffs own valid copyrights for the television programming at issue. The only question before the Court is whether Cablevision is "copying" plaintiffs' copyrighted programming or otherwise violating plaintiffs' rights under the Copyright Act.

Plaintiffs allege that Cablevision, through its RS-DVR, directly infringes upon their copyrights in two ways: one, Cablevision makes unauthorized copies of plaintiffs' programming, in violation of plaintiffs' right to reproduce their work; and two, Cablevision makes unauthorized transmissions of plaintiffs' programming, in violation of plaintiffs' exclusive right to publicly perform their work. I address each argument in turn.

1. *Is Cablevision Making Unauthorized Copies?*

According to plaintiffs, Cablevision makes multiple unauthorized copies of programming in two respects: (1) a complete copy of a program selected for recording is stored indefinitely on the customer's allotted hard drive space on the Arroyo server at Cablevision's facility; and (2) portions of programming are stored temporarily in buffer memory on Cablevision's servers.

i. *Arroyo Server Copies*

Cablevision does not deny that these copies are made in the operation of the RS-DVR, but, as the parties agree, the question is *who* makes the copies. Cablevision sees itself as entirely passive in the RS-DVR's recording process-it is the customer, Cablevision contends, who is "doing" the copying. To Cablevision, the RS-DVR is a machine, just like a VCR, STS-DVR, or a photocopier. Relying on *Sony* and other cases, Cablevision argues that it cannot be liable for copyright infringement for merely providing customers with the machinery to make copies. At most, it contends, its role with respect to the RS-DVR establishes indirect infringement, but plaintiffs have waived such a claim. Plaintiffs, on the other hand, allege direct infringement-that is, they claim that it is Cablevision that is "doing" the copying here. Plaintiffs characterize the RS-DVR as a service-one that requires the continuing and active involvement of Cablevision.

I agree with plaintiffs. The RS-DVR is clearly a service, and I hold that, in providing this service, it is Cablevision that does the copying.

In *Sony,* programming owners sued Sony and others for copyright infringement based on defendants' marketing and sale of Betamax VCRs. The record showed that consumers primarily used VCRs for home "time-shifting"-the practice of recording a program to view it at a later time, then erasing it. The Supreme Court held that time-shifting is "fair use" and does not violate the Copyright Act. The Court held that Sony's manufacture of Betamax VCRs therefore did not constitute contributory infringement.

Cablevision's reliance on *Sony* is misguided. . . . [A]part from their time-shifting functions, the RS-DVR and the VCR have little in common, and the relationship between Cablevision and potential RS-DVR customers is significantly different from the relationship between Sony and VCR users.

A VCR is a stand-alone piece of equipment. A consumer purchases the VCR and owns it outright. The consumer can then pick the VCR up, transport it, connect it to someone else's television and, assuming both devices are in working order, record programming. The RS-DVR does not have that stand-alone quality. An RS-DVR customer would not be able to disconnect his or her home set-top box, connect it elsewhere, and record programming. This is because the RS-DVR is not a single piece of equipment; it consists of a multitude of devices and processes. Unlike a VCR, the simple push of a button by the RS-DVR customer does not produce a recording. The pushing of the "record" button on the remote control merely sends a request to Cablevision's head-end to set the recording process in motion. The various computers and devices owned and operated by Cablevision and located at its head-end are needed to produce a recording.

Indeed, ownership of the RS-DVR set-top box remains with Cablevision and the RS-DVR requires a continuing relationship between Cablevision and its customers. In *Sony,* "[t]he only contact between Sony and the users of the Betamax . . . occurred at the moment of the sale." In stark contrast, Cablevision would not only supply a set-top box for the customer's home, but it would also decide which programming channels to make available for recording and provide that content, and it would house, operate, and maintain the rest of the equipment that makes the RS-DVR's recording process possible. Cablevision has physical control of the equipment at its head-end, and its personnel must monitor the programming streams at the head-end and ensure that the servers are working properly. Cablevision determines how much memory to allot to each customer and reserves storage capacity for each on a hard drive at its facility, and customers may very well be offered the option of acquiring additional capacity-for a fee. On the other hand, once Sony sells a VCR to a customer, Sony need not do anything further for the VCR to record.

The ongoing participation by Cablevision in the recording process also sets the RS-DVR apart from the STS-DVR. Cablevision claims that with both, the customer is "doing" the copying, and it points to the fact that no programmer . . . has ever sued Cablevision or any other cable operator in connection with its providing set-top storage DVRs to its customers. By extension, the RS-DVR, it argues, presents no copyright infringement.

This argument is unavailing. The fact that plaintiffs and other programming owners have not sued cable operators over the legality of STS-DVRs does not insulate the RS-DVR from such a challenge. Cablevision has not asserted any affirmative defenses to that effect, nor have plaintiffs conceded the legality of STS-DVRs. In any event, Cablevision's attempt to analogize the RS-DVR to the STS-DVR fails. The RS-DVR may have the look and feel of an STS-DVR, but "under the hood" the two types of DVRs are vastly different. For example, to effectuate the RS-DVR, Cablevision must reconfigure the linear channel programming signals received at its head-end by splitting the APS into a second stream, reformatting it through clamping, and routing it to the Arroyo servers. The STS-DVR does not require these activities. The STS-DVR can record directly to the hard drive located within the set-top box itself; it does not need the complex computer network and constant monitoring by Cablevision personnel necessary for the RS-DVR to record and store programming.

The RS-DVR, contrary to defendants' suggestions, is more akin to VOD than to a VCR, STS-DVR, or other time-shifting device. In fact, the RS-DVR is based on a modified VOD platform. With both systems, Cablevision decides what content to make available to customers for on-demand viewing. The programming available for viewing is stored outside the customer's home at Cablevision's head-end. Both utilize a "session resource manager," such as the eSRM used by the RS-DVR, to set up a temporary pathway to deliver programming in encrypted form to the customer for playback; decryption information is transmitted in both systems to the customer's set-top box. The number of available pathways for programming delivery in both systems is limited; if there are none available, the customer gets an error message or busy signal. Thus, in its architecture and delivery method, the RS-DVR bears striking resemblance to VOD-a service that Cablevision provides pursuant to licenses negotiated with programming owners.

NOTES AND QUESTIONS

1.   **VOD, VCR, S-DVR, and N-DVR.** The court evaluated the network DVR and classified it based on how the technology works, ruling it bore a close resemblance to video on demand (VOD) offerings and not to standard digital video recorder (S-DVR) options. From a functional perspective, however, customers would receive a service very similar to the S-DVR, but in a more technically efficient manner. Should the functional perspective matter to copyright law?

2.   **Computers and Copyright Law.** The court's formal judgment that the creation of a copy by the network DVR violated copyright law begs a question about digital computers: does a copy on any computer, even for a moment, create liability? If so, what other technologies—such as caching, which speeds up Internet content delivery by making a copy of the content closer to the end user—might also violate copyright law? How, if at all, is caching different from the network DVR?

Chapter 13:   Introduction to Telephone Regulation

See Chapter 20, below, for an excerpt from *Minnesota Public Utilities Commission v. FCC*, 483 F.3d 570 (8th Cir. 2007), which can also be read with the jurisdiction material ending on p. 712.

Chapter 17: Unbundling, Interconnection, and Related Issues

Insert the following just before Interconnection materials on p. 848:

The disputes surrounding unbundled network elements have settled down considerably in the wake of an evolving market, the resolution of the FCC's unbundling rules, and the changes to TELRIC pricing. Nonetheless, questions over the terms on which competitors can use incumbent networks have not gone away. On one hand, incumbents have used forbearance petitions to further reduce their obligations to unbundle network elements to competitors. Both Qwest and Alaska Communications Systems, for example, have received limited relief from unbundling obligations in Omaha and Anchorage, respectively, because of competition from facilities-based carriers. A discussion and order regarding the Alaska Communications Systems petition can be found at: http://www.fcc.gov/Daily_Releases/Daily_Business/2007/db0418/DA-07-1761A1.txt.

On the other hand, competitors have pushed for greater help from the FCC in procuring other facilities from ILECs. In 2006, the U.S. Government Accountability Office (GAO) issued a report that raised questions not about UNE access and pricing, but about "special access" pricing by incumbent carriers. Special access refers to dedicated, point-to-point facilities that incumbent carriers provide principally to large businesses and to other telecom carriers to use as parts of their networks. Special access facilities are generally used for high-capacity transport of calls and information by large customers. As contrasted with UNEs and switched access, special access prices have been subject to comparatively mild regulation. Recently, however, the FCC has received increased pressure to look again at special access and to impose stricter regulation on the terms upon which ILECs provide such facilities. In the words of FCC Commissioner Jonathan Adelstein:

> It is clear that many business customers and wholesale carriers rely heavily on the applicants' special access services for their voice and high-speed connections. Independent wireless companies, satellite providers, and long distance providers also depend on access to the applicants' nearly ubiquitous network and services to connect their networks to other carriers. In addition, many small rural providers depend on these services to connect to the Internet backbone. So, if the applicants were to raise prices as a result of diminished competition, such action would directly impact the cost and availability of services for large and small businesses, schools, hospitals, government offices, and independent wireless providers.

Concurring Statement of Commissioner Jonathan S. Adelstein, Re: AT&T Inc. and BellSouth Corporation Application for Transfer of Control, 22 FCC Rcd. 5662 (2006).

Adelstein's concern was sparked in part by merger activity (see the conditions on the AT&T-BellSouth merger, discussed below in the Chapter 21 material), but also by a Government Accounting Office (GAO) report from November 2006 that raised concerns about performance of the special access market. (See the report at http://www.gao.gov/new.items/d0780.pdf.). Special access regulation is therefore likely to be a salient regulatory issue in the near future, as the AT&T-BellSouth merger conditions demonstrate.

Inter-carrier compensation and access charges.

The next two excerpts are to be inserted at p. 860 after the excerpt on unified inter-carrier compensation reform; they are also relevant to the access charge materials at the end of Chapter 18.

Blocking of Free-Conference-Call Services. In April 2007, several large carriers, notably large wireless carriers like AT&T/Cingular, acknowledged that they were blocking calls to certain free (to end-user consumers) conference calling services. FCC Chair Kevin Martin responded to this admission by warning the blocking carriers that unless they stopped blocking the calls, the FCC "would end up taking action as we saw necessary." The carriers at issue quickly agreed to stop blocking calls to the services at issue, but they have continued to pursue actions against such services. Why? Because, according to the blocking carriers, such services make their money by taking improper advantage of the current inter-carrier compensation regime. Some free conferencing services work by routing their calls through small, local telephone exchanges in Iowa, hence the 712 area codes for those calls. The local, rural carriers through which the conference call services work charge termination fees (which include a number of subsidies) to the networks carrying the incoming calls. The terminating rural carriers then share these fees with the conference-call service provider. In this way consumers pay nothing, but the networks that originate calls to the "free" services pay substantial fees (which they typically do not or cannot pass through to consumers) that generate profits both for the conference-call service provider and the rural network that terminates its incoming calls.

AT&T and other carriers, while apparently no longer blocking calls to the services at issue, have filed lawsuits and complaints to the FCC against the rural carriers in Iowa alleging that their deals with the conference-call services are scams that violate FCC rules and other laws. The FCC has made clear that while it will entertain those petitions, the allegedly injured carriers cannot block consumers' ability to reach the conference-call services in the interim. As the FCC continues with its review of intercarrier compensation generally, more specific disputes are thus underway and likely to be the subject of Commission proceedings in the near future.

Time Warner Cable Request for Declaratory Ruling that Competitive Local Exchange Carriers May Obtain Interconnection Under Section 251 of the Communications Act to Provide Wholesale Telecommunications Services to VoIP Providers, Memorandum Opinion and Order
22 FCC Rcd. 3513 (2007)

By the Chief, Wireline Competition Bureau:

INTRODUCTION

     1. In this Order, the Wireline Competition Bureau (Bureau) grants a petition for declaratory ruling filed by Time Warner Cable (TWC) asking the Commission to declare that wholesale telecommunications carriers are entitled to interconnect and exchange traffic with incumbent local exchange carriers (LECs) when providing services to other service providers, including voice over Internet Protocol (VoIP) service providers pursuant to sections 251(a) and (b) of the Communications Act of 1934, as amended (the Act). As explained below, we reaffirm that wholesale providers of telecommunications services are telecommunications carriers for the purposes of sections 251(a) and (b) of the Act, and are entitled to the rights of

telecommunications carriers under that provision. We conclude that state commission decisions denying wholesale telecommunications service providers the right to interconnect with incumbent LECs pursuant to sections 251(a) and (b) of the Act are inconsistent with the Act and Commission precedent and would frustrate the development of competition and broadband deployment.

BACKGROUND

E.   TWC's Petition

2.   On March 1, 2006, TWC filed a petition for declaratory ruling requesting that the Commission affirm that "requesting wholesale telecommunications carriers are entitled to obtain interconnection with incumbent LECs to provide wholesale telecommunications services to other service providers" (including VoIP-based providers). In its Petition, TWC states that in 2003 it began to deploy a facilities-based competitive telephone service using VoIP technology, which enables it to offer a combined package of video, high-speed data, and voice services. TWC purchases wholesale telecommunications services from certain telecommunications carriers, including MCI WorldCom Network Services Inc. (MCI) and Sprint Communications Company, L.P. (Sprint), to connect TWC's VoIP service customers with the public switched telephone network (PSTN). MCI and Sprint provide transport for the origination and termination on the PSTN through their interconnection agreements with incumbent LECs. In addition, MCI and Sprint provide TWC with connectivity to the incumbent's E911 network and other necessary components as a wholesale service.

3.   TWC claims that MCI has been unable to provide wholesale telecommunications services to TWC in certain areas in South Carolina and that Sprint has been unable to provide wholesale telecommunications services to TWC in certain areas in Nebraska because, unlike certain other state commissions, the South Carolina Public Service Commission (South Carolina Commission) and the Nebraska Public Service Commission (Nebraska Commission) have determined that rural incumbent LECs are not obligated to enter into interconnection agreements with competitive service providers (like MCI and Sprint) to the extent that such competitors operate as wholesale service providers. TWC argues that the South Carolina and Nebraska Commissions misinterpreted the statute when they decided, among other things, that competitive LECs providing wholesale telecommunications services to other service providers, in this case VoIP-based providers, are not "telecommunications carriers" for the purposes of section 251 of the Act, and, therefore, are not entitled to interconnect with incumbent LECs.

4. TWC asks the Commission to grant a declaratory ruling reaffirming that telecommunications carriers are entitled to obtain interconnection with incumbent LECs to provide wholesale telecommunications services to other service providers. The Petition also requests that the Commission clarify that interconnection rights under section 251 of the Act are not based on the identity of the wholesale carrier's customer.

State Commission Decisions

5. *South Carolina.* On October 8, 2004, MCI initiated interconnection negotiations pursuant to section 252(a) of the Act with four rural incumbent LECs operating in South Carolina. These rural incumbent LECs claimed that they were not required to accept traffic from a third-party provider that purchases wholesale telecommunications services from MCI. On March 17, 2005, MCI filed a petition with the South Carolina Commission seeking arbitration of the unresolved issues between MCI and the rural incumbent LECs. In arbitrating this dispute, the

South Carolina Commission agreed with the rural incumbent LECs that the arbitrated interconnection agreement should be limited to the traffic generated by the rural incumbent LECs' customers and MCI's direct end-user customers on their respective networks. The South Carolina Commission determined that MCI is not entitled to seek interconnection with the rural incumbent LECs with respect to the wholesale services MCI proposed to provide to TWC because such wholesale service does not meet the definition of "telecommunications service" under the Act and, therefore, MCI is not a "telecommunications carrier" with respect to those services. The South Carolina Commission also found that section 251(b) obligations "relate to parallel obligations between two competing telecommunications carriers" and that MCI's intent to act as an "intermediary for a facilities-based VoIP service provider" is a type of non-parallel relationship not contemplated or provided for under the Act.

6. *Nebraska.* On December 16, 2004, Sprint commenced interconnection negotiations with Southeast Nebraska Telephone Company (SENTCO), a rural incumbent LEC, pursuant to section 252(a) of the Act. In its September 13, 2005 arbitration decision, the Nebraska Commission determined that Sprint is not a "telecommunications carrier" under the *NARUC I* and *Virgin Islands* test for common carriage because the relationship between Sprint and TWC is an "individually negotiated and tailored, private business arrangement" that is an untariffed offering to a sole user of this service, and, therefore, Sprint cannot assert any rights under sections 251 and 252 of the Act. In addition, the Nebraska Commission held that because TWC operates the switch that "directly serves the called party," Sprint was not entitled to exercise rights under section 251(b).

7. *Other State Proceedings.* TWC asserts that, in contrast to the South Carolina and Nebraska decisions, public utility commissions in Illinois, Iowa, New York and Ohio have recognized that wholesale service providers, such as Sprint and MCI, are telecommunications carriers with rights under section 251 of the Act. In addition, TWC and other commenters point to other state commissions that have before them pending proceedings on this same issue.

DISCUSSION

8. The Bureau grants TWC's request to the extent described below. Because the Act does not differentiate between retail and wholesale services when defining "telecommunications carrier" or "telecommunications service," we clarify that telecommunications carriers are entitled to interconnect and exchange traffic with incumbent LECs pursuant to section 251(a) and (b) of the Act for the purpose of providing wholesale telecommunications services. The Bureau finds that a contrary decision would impede the important development of wholesale telecommunications and facilities-based VoIP competition, as well as broadband deployment policies developed and implemented by the Commission over the last decade, by limiting the ability of wholesale carriers to offer service.

"Telecommunications Service" Can Be Either a Wholesale or Retail Service

9. Consistent with Commission precedent, we find that the Act does not differentiate between the provision of telecommunications services on a wholesale or retail basis for the purposes of sections 251(a) and (b), and we confirm that providers of wholesale telecommunications services enjoy the same rights as any "telecommunications carrier" under those provisions of the Act. We further conclude that the statutory classification of the end-user service, and the classification of VoIP specifically, is not dispositive of the wholesale carrier's rights under section 251.

10. The Act defines "telecommunications" to mean "the transmission, between or among points specified by the user, of information of the user's choosing, without change in the form or content of the information as sent and received." The Act defines "telecommunications service" to mean "the offering of telecommunications for a fee directly to the public, or to such classes of users as to be effectively available directly to the public, regardless of the facilities used." Finally, any provider of telecommunications services is a "telecommunications carrier" by definition under the Act.

11. It is clear under the Commission's precedent that the definition of "telecommunications services" is not limited to retail services, but also includes wholesale services when offered on a common carrier basis. The South Carolina Commission's contrary interpretation—that services provided on a wholesale basis to carriers or other providers are not telecommunications services because they are not offered "directly to the public" has been expressly rejected by the Commission in the past, as we explain below.

12. The definition of "telecommunications services" in the Act does not specify whether those services are "retail" or "wholesale," but merely specifies that "telecommunications" be offered for a fee "directly to the public, or to such classes of users as to be effectively available directly to the public." In *NARUC II*, the D.C. Circuit stated that "[t]his does not mean that the particular services offered must practically be available to the entire public; a specialized carrier whose service is of possible use to only a fraction of the population may nonetheless be a common carrier if he holds himself out to serve indifferently all potential users." Thus, the question at issue in this proceeding is whether the relevant wholesale telecommunications "services" are offered "directly to the public, or to such classes of users as to be effectively available directly to the public." Indeed, the definition of "telecommunications services" long has been held to include both retail and wholesale services under Commission precedent. In the *Non-Accounting Safeguards Order*, the Commission concluded that wholesale services are included in the definition of "telecommunications service." . . . The Commission affirmed these conclusions in the *Non-Accounting Safeguards Reconsideration Order* where it found "no basis in the statute, legislative history, or FCC precedent for finding the reference to 'the public' in the statutory definition to be intended to exclude wholesale telecommunications services."

13. We further find that our decision today is consistent with and will advance the Commission's goals in promoting facilities-based competition as well as broadband deployment. Apart from encouraging competition for wholesale services in their own right, ensuring the protections of section 251 interconnection is a critical component for the growth of facilities-based local competition. Moreover, as the Commission has recognized most recently in the *VoIP 911 Order*, VoIP is often accessed over broadband facilities, and there is a nexus between the availability of VoIP services and the goals of section 706 of the Act. Furthermore, as the Petition and some commenters note, in that order the Commission expressly contemplated that VoIP providers would obtain access to and interconnection with the PSTN through competitive carriers. Therefore, we also rely on section 706 as a basis for our determination today that affirming the rights of wholesale carriers to interconnect for the purpose of exchanging traffic with VoIP providers will spur the development of broadband infrastructure. We further conclude that such wholesale competition and its facilitation of the introduction of new technology holds particular promise for consumers in rural areas.

14. In making this clarification, we emphasize that the rights of telecommunications carriers to section 251 interconnection are limited to those carriers that, at a minimum, do in fact provide telecommunications services to their customers, either on a wholesale or retail basis. We do not address or express any opinion on any state commission's evidentiary assessment of the

facts before it in an arbitration or other proceeding regarding whether a carrier offers a telecommunications service. However, we make clear that the rights of telecommunications carriers under sections 251 (a) and (b) apply regardless of whether the telecommunications services are wholesale or retail, and a state decision to the contrary is inconsistent with the Act and Commission precedent.

F.   The Section 251 (a) and (b) Rights of a Wholesale Telecommunications Carrier Do Not Depend on the Regulatory Classification of the Retail Service Offered to the End User

15. As explained above, a provider of wholesale telecommunications service is a telecommunications carrier and is entitled to interconnection under section 251 of the Act. The regulatory classification of the service provided to the ultimate end user has no bearing on the wholesale provider's rights as a telecommunications carrier to interconnect under section 251. As such, we clarify that the statutory classification of a third-party provider's VoIP service as an information service or a telecommunications service is irrelevant to the issue of whether a wholesale provider of telecommunications may seek interconnection under section 251(a) and (b). Thus, we need not, and do not, reach here the issues raised in the *IP-Enabled Services* docket, including the statutory classification of VoIP services. We thus reject the arguments that the regulatory status of VoIP is the underlying issue in this matter or that Commission action on this Petition will prejudge issues raised in the *IP-Enabled Services* docket. We also make clear that we do not address any entitlement of a retail service provider to serve end users through such a wholesale arrangement, nor, contrary to the views of some commenters, do we read the Petition to seek such rights. Rather, in issuing this decision, we reiterate that we only find that a carrier is entitled to interconnect with another carrier pursuant to sections 251(a) and (b) in order to provide wholesale telecommunications service.

16. Finally, we emphasize that our ruling today is limited to telecommunications carriers that provide wholesale telecommunications service and that seek interconnection *in their own right* for the purpose of transmitting traffic to or from another service provider. To address concerns by commenters about which parties are eligible to assert these rights, we make clear that the scope of our declaratory ruling is limited to wholesale carriers that are acting as telecommunications carrier for purposes of their interconnection request. In affirming the rights of wholesale carriers, we also make clear that today's decision in no way diminishes the ongoing obligations of these wholesalers as telecommunications carriers, including compliance with any technical requirements imposed by this Commission or a state commission. In addition, we agree that it is most consistent with Commission policy that where a LEC wins back a customer from a VoIP provider, the number should be ported to the LEC that wins the customer at the customer's request, and therefore we make such a requirement an explicit condition to the section 251 rights provided herein. Other concerns about porting will be addressed in the *IP-Enabled Services* proceeding.

G.   Other Issues Raised by Commenters

Certain commenters ask us to reach other issues, including the application of section 251(b)(5) and the classification of VoIP services. We do not find it appropriate or necessary here to resolve the complex issues surrounding the interpretation of Title II more generally or the subsections of section 251 more specifically that the Commission is currently addressing elsewhere on more comprehensive records. For example, the question concerning the proper statutory classification of VoIP remains pending in the *IP-Enabled Services* docket. Moreover, in this declaratory ruling proceeding we do not find it appropriate to revisit any state commission's evidentiary assessment of whether an entity demonstrated that it held itself out to the public sufficiently to be deemed a common carrier under well-established case law. In the particular wholesale/retail provider relationship described by Time Warner in the instant petition, the wholesale telecommunications carriers have assumed responsibility for compensating the incumbent LEC for the termination of traffic under a section 251 arrangement between those two parties. We make such an arrangement an explicit condition to the section 251 rights provided herein. We do not, however, prejudge the Commission's determination of what compensation is appropriate, or any other issues pending in the *Intercarrier Compensation* docket.

NOTES AND QUESTIONS

1. **The Ghost of Intercarrier Compensation.** The Time Warner decision and the call blocking issue discussed above both purport to be about interconnection. In fact, however, concerns about intercarrier compensation—or lack thereof—underpin the disputes in both cases. In the Time Warner case, the rural telephone companies were concerned that, to the extent calls were traveling to and from Voice over IP providers, those providers would not pay the same amount as traditional providers. In the call blocking case, the traditional providers resented delivering calls to rural carriers who were serving the conferencing service. In both cases, denial of interconnection was a self-help remedy. Should this remedy be permitted? If it was, what would be the consequence?

2. **Wholesale v. Retail.** In most cases, Voice over IP providers contract with established firms to provide transport connectivity and interconnection. (In many cases, they also will contract for numbers, emergency 911 support, and other services.) From a legal perspective, Voice over IP providers take the position that they are not "telecommunications carriers," but rather customers of telecommunications carriers. If Voice over IP providers are only customers, and have no legal standing to request interconnection on their own right, should they be entitled to obtain interconnection derivatively through other telecommunications carriers? How about phone numbers?

3. **Deciding Not to Decide.** As we discuss below in Chapter 20 (at p. 1047 and relevant supplemental materials), the FCC has yet to decide whether Voice over IP is a "telecommunications service" or an "information service." If Voice over IP providers were telecommunications service providers, their right to interconnection would be indisputable. Why have they not embraced that position? Why has the FCC stalled on deciding their legal status?

Chapter 18:   Universal Service and Access Charges

Insert at p. 880, just before the section on access charge reform:

High-Cost Universal Service Support
FCC 07J-1, 2007 WL 1288121 (May 1, 2007)

By the Federal-State Joint Board on Universal Service:

IV.   INTRODUCTION

1.   In this Recommended Decision, the Federal-State Joint Board on Universal Service (Joint Board) recommends that the Commission take immediate action to rein in the explosive growth in high-cost universal service support disbursements. Specifically, we recommend that the Commission impose an interim, emergency cap on the amount of high-cost support that competitive eligible telecommunications carriers (ETCs) may receive for each state based on the average level of competitive ETC support distributed in that state in 2006. We also recommend that the Joint Board and the Commission further explore comprehensive high-cost distribution reform. As part of that effort, today in a companion Public Notice we seek comment on various proposals to reform the high-cost universal service support mechanisms. We also commit to making further recommendations regarding comprehensive high-cost universal service reform within six months of this Recommended Decision. Finally, we recommend that the Commission act on these further recommendations within one year from the date of our further recommended decision.

V.   BACKGROUND

2.   In 2002, the Commission asked the Joint Board to review certain of the Commission's rules related to the high-cost universal service support mechanisms. Among other things, the Commission asked the Joint Board to review the Commission's rules relating to high-cost universal service support in study areas in which a competitive ETC is providing service. In response, the Joint Board made many recommendations concerning the designation of ETCs in high-cost areas, but declined to recommend that the Commission modify the basis of support (*i.e.*, the methodology used to calculate support) in study areas with multiple ETCs. Instead, the Joint Board recommended that it and the Commission consider possible modifications to the basis of support for competitive ETCs as part of an overall review of the high-cost support mechanisms for rural and non-rural carriers.

3.   In 2004, the Commission asked the Joint Board to review the Commission's rules relating to the high-cost universal service support mechanisms for rural carriers and to determine the appropriate rural mechanism to succeed the plan adopted in the *Rural Task Force Order*. In August 2004, the Joint Board sought comment on issues the Commission referred to it related to the high-cost universal service support mechanisms for rural carriers. The Joint Board also specifically sought comment on the methodology for calculating support for ETCs in competitive study areas. Since that time, the Joint Board has sought comment on a variety of specific proposals for addressing the issues of universal service support for rural carriers and the basis of support for competitive ETCs, including proposals developed by members and staff of the Joint Board and the use of reverse auctions (competitive bidding) to determine high-cost universal service funding to ETCs.

VI. RECOMMENDATION FOR AN IMMEDIATE INTERIM CAP ON SUPPORT FOR COMPETITIVE ELIGIBLE TELECOMMUNICATIONS CARRIERS

A. Need for Immediate Action

4.   High-cost support has been rapidly increasing in recent years and, without immediate action to restrain growth in competitive ETC funding, the federal universal service fund is in dire jeopardy of becoming unsustainable. Today, the universal service fund provides approximately $4 billion per year in high-cost support. Yet, in 2001 high-cost support totaled approximately $2.6 billion. In recent years, this growth has been due to increased support provided to competitive ETCs which receive high-cost support based on the per-line support that the incumbent local exchange carriers (LECs) receive rather than the competitive ETC's own costs. While support to incumbent LECs has been flat or even declined since 2003, by contrast, in the six years from 2001 through 2006, competitive ETC support grew from $15 million to almost $1 billion—an annual growth rate of over 100 percent. Based on current estimates, competitive ETC support in 2007 will reach at least $1.28 billion if the Commission takes no action to curtail this growth. Moreover, if the Commission were now to approve all competitive ETC petitions currently pending before the Commission, high-cost support for competitive ETCs could rise to as much as $1.56 billion in 2007. High-cost support to competitive ETCs is estimated to grow to almost $2 billion in 2008 and $2.5 billion in 2009 even without additional competitive ETC designations in 2008 and 2009.

5.   We conclude that immediate action must be taken to stem the dramatic growth in high-cost support. We therefore recommend that the Commission immediately impose an interim cap on high-cost support provided to competitive ETCs until such measures can be adopted that will ensure that the fund will be sustainable for future years. We believe that taking this action will prevent increases in high-cost support due to the designation of additional competitive ETCs or line growth among existing competitive ETCs. While imposition of the interim cap will not address the current disproportionate distribution of competitive ETC support among the states, the cap will stop growth in competitive ETC support while the Joint Board and the Commission consider fundamental reforms to address issues related to the distribution of support. At this time, we do not recommend additional caps on support provided to incumbent LECs, because the data show less growth pressure from incumbent LECs. Moreover, incumbent LEC high-cost loop support is already capped and incumbent interstate access support has a targeted limit. Also, local switching support and interstate common line support provided to incumbent LECs have been stable in recent years. Accordingly, we recommend that the Commission immediately impose an interim high-cost support cap, but one that is limited to high-cost support provided to competitive ETCs.

6.   We believe that adopting an interim cap on high-cost support only for competitive ETCs would not violate the Commission's universal service principle of competitive neutrality for several reasons. Fundamental differences exist between the regulatory treatment of competitive ETCs and incumbent LECs. For example, competitive ETCs, unlike incumbent LECs, have no equal access obligations. Competitive ETCs also are not subject to rate regulation. In addition, competitive ETCs may not have the same carrier of last resort obligations that incumbent LECs have. Furthermore, under the identical support rule, both incumbent rural LECs and competitive ETCs receive support based on the incumbent rural LECs' costs. Therefore, incumbent rural LECs' support is cost-based, while competitive ETCs' support is not. Due to this, as discussed below, we recommend that the Commission consider abandoning the identical support rule in any comprehensive and fundamental reform ultimately adopted.

7.   We decline to recommend that the Commission adopt General Communication Inc.'s (GCI) proposal that we exempt wireline competitive ETCs from the cap. The growth of support to wireless competitive ETCs may indeed have been much greater than the growth of support to wireline competitive ETCs. However, we recommend a cap today largely because we conclude that the identical support rule has become dated and may no longer be the most appropriate approach to calculating support for competitive ETCs. Today wireline competitive ETCs (such as GCI) and wireless competitive ETCs both derive their universal service support from the identical support rule. Neither receives support based on its own costs. In addition, GCI would have us create an exemption based upon the ETC's chosen technology, rather than its legal status. We are not aware of anything in the Commission's current rules that provides a precedent for such a technology-based differentiation within universal service policy.

B.   Length of Time

8.   We emphasize that the cap on competitive ETC support that we recommend here should be an interim measure that is used to stem the growing crisis in high-cost support growth while the Commission and the Joint Board consider further reform. We remain committed to comprehensive reform of the high-cost universal service support mechanisms. Accordingly, we recommend that the Commission immediately adopt an interim cap on high-cost support to competitive ETCs, and that the cap expire one year from the date of any Joint Board recommended decision on comprehensive and fundamental universal service reform. As discussed below, we commit to adoption of a further recommended decision addressing fundamental high cost reforms within six months of today's Recommended Decision. We also anticipate that the Commission will act promptly on the Joint Board's subsequent recommended decision in light of the interim nature of the cap, notwithstanding the fact that the Communications Act of 1934, as amended (the Act) imposes a one-year time limit on such action.

C.   Operation of the Cap

9.   We recommend that the Commission immediately impose a cap on competitive ETC support for each state. We believe that a competitive ETC cap applied at a state level effectively curbs growth but allows states some flexibility to direct competitive ETC support to the areas in the state that are most in need of such support. An interim, state-based cap on competitive ETC support will also avoid creating an incentive for each state to designate as many new ETCs as possible. A state-based cap will require newly designated competitive ETCs to share funding with other competitive ETCs within the state.

NOTES AND QUESTIONS

1.   **Reverse Auctions.** In August 2006, the Federal-State Joint Board on Universal Service sought comment on the use of reverse auctions to allocate universal service support. With reverse auctions, eligible carriers would bid for the universal service obligation and accompanying high-cost support for a given area over a specified time period. The assignment would go to the carrier that bids the lowest subsidy to provide service of the required quality. As the excerpt above indicates, the Joint Board is considering using reverse auctions to limit the growth of the high-cost fund by improving accountability and efficiency. Because the auctions would limit the number of supported networks and select the most cost-effective bids, reverse auctions could reduce the total amount of high-cost support.

2.   **Gaming.** Does the Board's recommended decision indicate that ETCs are gaming the universal service system? Abusing it? If so, who is at fault? The ETCs? The states? Those who

created the rules?

3.   Broadband.   At present, the universal service fund does not provide any support for broadband. Should it? Is the growth of ETC support—largely for wireless carriers in relatively densely populated areas—an appropriate emphasis as opposed to the lack of support for broadband? What type of subsidy program, if any, should be implemented for broadband— should it subsidize multiple carriers, should it be limited to certain areas, and who should administer it?

4.   Long Term. The Board has recommended a temporary step. What is a good long-term solution? What goals should such a solution embrace with respect to the traditionally protected "rural carriers" (i.e., smaller independent firms not part of larger carriers who are subject to price cap regulation).

Chapter 19:   The Internet

The following is the lower court opinion on remand after *Ashcroft v. ACLU*, **542 U.S. 656 (2004), which is on page 936 of the casebook. This opinion should be inserted after** *Ashcroft*:

ACLU, et al. v. ALBERTO R. GONZALES
478 F. Supp. 2d 775 (E.D.PA., 2007)

Reed, Senior District Judge:

At issue in this case is the constitutionality of the Child Online Protection Act, 47 U.S.C. §231 ("COPA") and whether this court should issue a permanent injunction against its enforcement due to its alleged constitutional infirmities. COPA provides both criminal and civil penalties for transmitting sexually explicit materials and communications over the World Wide Web ("Web") which are available to minors and harmful to them. 47 U.S.C. §231(a). After a trial on the merits, for the reasons that follow, notwithstanding the compelling interest of Congress in protecting children from sexually explicit material on the Web, I conclude today that COPA facially violates the First and Fifth Amendment rights of the plaintiffs because: (1) at least some of the plaintiffs have standing; (2) COPA is not narrowly tailored to Congress' compelling interest; (3) defendant has failed to meet his burden of showing that COPA is the least restrictive, most effective alternative in achieving the compelling interest; and (3) COPA is impermissibly vague and overbroad. As a result, I will issue a permanent injunction against the enforcement of COPA.

II. THE RELEVANT LANGUAGE OF COPA AND THE CONSTITUTION

COPA provides that:

> Whoever knowingly and with knowledge of the character of the material, in interstate or foreign commerce by means of the World Wide Web, makes any communication for commercial purposes that is available to any minor and that includes any material that is harmful to minors shall be fined not more than $50,000, imprisoned not more than 6 months, or both.

47 U.S.C. §231(a)(1). There is an additional monetary penalty for intentional violations of the above quoted language and a provision for additional civil penalties. 47 U.S.C. §231(a)(2) & (3).

The crux of the statute is found in the definition of "harmful to minors" which tracks the familiar *Miller* obscenity standard. *See Miller v. California,* 413 U.S. 15, 24 (1973). Specifically, "material that is harmful to minors", means:

> any communication, picture, image, graphic image file, article, recording, writing, or other matter of any kind that is obscene or that—
>
> (A) the average person, applying contemporary community standards, would find, taking the material as a whole and with respect to minors, is designed to appeal to, or is designed to pander to, the prurient interest;
>
> (B) depicts, describes, or represents, in a manner patently offensive with respect to minors, an actual or simulated sexual act or sexual contact, an actual or simulated

normal or perverted sexual act, or a lewd exhibition of the genitals or post-pubescent female breast; and

(C) taken as a whole, lacks serious literary, artistic, political, or scientific value for minors.

47 U.S.C. §231(e)(6). A minor is defined as "any person under 17 years of age." 47 U.S.C. §231(e)(7).

"[B]y means of the World Wide Web" is defined as the "placement of material in a computer server-based file archive so that it is publicly accessible, over the Internet, using hypertext transfer protocol [("HTTP")] or any successor protocol." 47 U.S.C. §231(e)(1). Under COPA, the Internet "means the combination of computer facilities and electromagnetic transmission media, and related equipment and software, comprising the interconnected worldwide network of computer networks that employ the Transmission Control Protocol/Internet Protocol or any successor protocol to transmit information." 47 U.S.C. §231(e)(3).

Another important feature of COPA for the purposes of this action is that "[a] person shall be considered to make a communication for commercial purposes only if such person is engaged in the business of making such communication." 47 U.S.C. §231(e)(2)(A). Moreover, "engaged in the business" means that:

> the person who makes a communication, or offers to make a communication, by means of the World Wide Web, that includes any material that is harmful to minors, devotes time, attention, or labor to such activities, as a regular course of such person's trade or business, with the objective of earning a profit as a result of such activities (although it is not necessary that the person make a profit or that the making or offering to make such communications be the person's sole or principal business or source of income). A person may be considered to be engaged in the business of making, by means of the World Wide Web, communications for commercial purposes that include material that is harmful to minors, only if the person knowingly causes the material that is harmful to minors to be posted on the World Wide Web or knowingly solicits such material to be posted on the World Wide Web.

47 U.S.C. §231(e)(2)(B).

Although COPA brands all speech falling within its reach as criminal speech, it also provides an affirmative defense against liability if:

> the defendant, in good faith, has restricted access by minors to material that is harmful to minors—
>
> (A) by requiring use of a credit card, debit account, adult access code, or adult personal identification number;
>
> (B) by accepting a digital certificate that verifies age; or
>
> (C) by any other reasonable measures that are feasible under available technology.

47 U.S.C. §231(c)(1).

Moreover, those exempt from liability include telecommunications carriers, Internet access service providers, those engaged in the business of providing an Internet information location tool, or those:

> similarly engaged in the transmission, storage, retrieval, hosting, formatting, or translation (or any combination thereof) of a communication made by another person, without selection or alteration of the content of the communication, except that such person's deletion of a particular communication or material made by another person in a manner consistent with subsection (c) of this section or section 230 of this title shall not constitute such selection or alteration of the content of the communication.

47 U.S.C. §231(b).

III. Findings of Fact

[The court made findings, *inter alia,* that, while some mechanisms of blocking access by minors to sexually explicit material (e.g. credit card requirements) were of questionable effect, filtering technology is effective and generally blocks 95% of sexually explicit material.]

G. Select Legislative History of COPA and the Limitations of COPA

122. According to House Report 105-775, "[t]he purpose of [COPA] is to amend the Communications Act of 1934 by prohibiting the sale of pornographic materials on the World Wide Web (or the Web) to minors." H.R. Rep. 105-775, at *5.

123. The intended "effect of [COPA] is simply to reorder the process in such a way as to require age verification before pornography is made available, essentially requiring the commercial pornographer to put sexually explicit images 'behind the counter.'" *Id.* at *15.

124. The House Report also lists the following Congressional findings:

> (1) while custody, care, and nurture of the child resides first with the parent, the widespread availability of the Internet presents opportunities for minors to access materials through the World Wide Web in a manner that can frustrate parental supervision or control;

> (2) the protection of the physical and psychological well-being of minors by shielding them from materials that are harmful to them is a compelling governmental interest;

> (3) to date, while the industry has developed innovative ways to help parents and educators restrict material that is harmful to minors through parental control protections and self-regulation, such efforts have not provided a national solution to the problem of minors accessing harmful material on the World Wide Web;

> (4) a prohibition on the distribution of material harmful to minors, combined with legitimate defenses, is currently the most effective means by which to satisfy the compelling government interest; and

> (5) notwithstanding the existence of protections that limit the distribution over the World Wide Web of material that is harmful to minors, parents, educators, and industry must continue efforts to protect children from dangers posed by the Internet.

Id. at *2.

125. COPA was drafted in direct response to the Supreme Court's decision in *Reno,* 521 U.S. 844regarding the CDA. *Id.* at *5.

126. COPA's reach is specifically limited only to files publically accessible over the Web via HTTP or a successor protocol and does not reach other forms of communication and data transfer over the Internet including email, newsgroups, message boards, peer-to-peer and other file sharing networks, chat, instant messaging, VoIP, and FTP. 47 U.S.C. §231(e)(1); H.R. Rep. 105-775, at *12.

127. Congress added this limitation in an attempt to not burden more speech than was necessary and to attempt to ensure that COPA was narrowly tailored, unlike the CDA. H.R. Rep. 105-775, at *12.

128. COPA does not apply to Web sites which are completely free and which do not fit within the definitions of "commercial purposes" and "engaged in the business." 47 U.S.C. §231(e)(2).

129. This limitation was specifically added by Congress to address the Supreme Court's concern that the CDA was too broad in that it covered both commercial and noncommercial speech. H.R. Rep. 105-775, at *8, *12.

IV. CONCLUSIONS OF LAW

C. Defendant Has Failed to Meet His Burden of Proof

1. Defendant Has Failed to Show that COPA Is Narrowly Tailored to Congress' Compelling Interest

a. COPA Is Overinclusive

9. COPA is overinclusive. Due to the broad definitions and provisions of COPA, COPA prohibits much more speech than is necessary to further Congress' compelling interest. For example, the definitions of "commercial purposes" and "engaged in the business" apply to an inordinate amount of Internet speech and certainly cover more than just commercial pornographers, contrary to the claim of defendant. Moreover, the fact that COPA applies to speech that is obscene as to all minors from newborns to age sixteen, and not just to speech that is obscene as to older minors, also renders COPA over-inclusive.

b. COPA Is Underinclusive

10. COPA is also underinclusive. For example, as shown in Findings of Fact 63, 65, and 66, there is a significant amount of sexually explicit material on the Internet which originates from outside of the United States. As discussed below, unlike Internet content filters which are able to block from view unsuitable material regardless of its origin (*see* Finding of Fact 80), COPA has no extra-territorial application. As a result, and as is more fully discussed below, COPA is not applicable to a large amount of material that is unsuitable for children which originates overseas but is nevertheless available to children in the United States.

13. As shown in Finding of Fact 130, the legislative history of COPA does not support a finding that Congress intended for COPA to apply to Web sites that are hosted or registered outside of the United States and instead shows that Congress intended for the statute to have only domestic application. *See also* H.R. Rep. 105-775, at *20.

14. If Congress had intended for COPA to have extraterritorial application, it could have inserted appropriate language in the statute.

16. As demonstrated in Finding of Fact 126, it is also accurate that COPA only concerns itself with material that is accessible over the Internet using HTTP or a successor protocol. As advocated by the plaintiffs, it appears that this is yet another reason why COPA is underinclusive. However, the compelling interest of Congress, as submitted by defendant, is quite narrow in that it seeks only to protect children form harmful materials on the *Web*. Therefore, I will restrict my analysis to materials available on the Web and will not consider the ramifications of COPA's failure to reach other harmful materials on the Internet accessible by means other than the Web.

c. The Affirmative Defenses in COPA Do Not Aid in Narrowly Tailoring It to Congress' Compelling Interest

17. The affirmative defenses cannot cure COPA's failure to be narrowly tailored because they are effectively unavailable. Credit cards, debit accounts, adult access codes, and adult personal identification numbers do not in fact verify age. As a result, their use does not, "in good faith," "restrict[] access" by minors. 47 U.S.C. §231(c)(1)(A); *see* Findings of Fact 137, 138, 140-147, 148-158, 159-160.

21. The affirmative defenses also raise their own First Amendment concerns. For example, the utilization of those devices to trigger COPA's affirmative defenses will deter listeners, many of whom will be unwilling to reveal personal and financial information in order to access content and, thus, will chill speech. *See Denver Area Educ. Telecomms. Consortium, Inc. v FCC*, 518 U.S. 727, 754 (1996) (striking down an identification requirement because it would "further restrict viewing by subscribers who fear for their reputations should the operator, advertently or inadvertently, disclose the list of those who wish to watch the 'patently offensive' channel"); Findings of Fact 171, 172-181.

22. Similarly, the affirmative defenses also impermissibly burden Web site operators with demonstrating that their speech is lawful. *See Ashcroft v. Free Speech Coalition*, 535 U.S. 234, 255 (2002) (stating that "The Government raises serious constitutional difficulties by seeking to impose on the defendant the burden of proving his speech is not unlawful"); *ACLU v. Ashcroft*, 322 F.3d 240, 260 (3d Cir. 2003) (noting that "the affirmative defenses [in COPA] do not provide the Web publishers with assurances of freedom from prosecution"). Under the COPA regime, Web site operators are unable to defend themselves until after they are prosecuted. *See* 47 U.S.C. §231(c).

23. Moreover, the affirmative defenses place substantial economic burdens on the exercise of protected speech because all of them involve significant cost and the loss of Web site visitors, especially to those plaintiffs who provide their content for free. Findings of Fact 161-163, 165-171. Defendant's response to this proposition, that the defenses are not burdensome to commercial pornographers because they already accept credit cards to sell their content, shows his fundamental misunderstanding of the reach of COPA: COPA does not apply merely to commercial pornographers but to a wide range of speakers on the Web.

25. As shown above, the affirmative defenses in COPA raise unique First Amendment issues and, in any event, do not aid in narrowly tailoring COPA to Congress' compelling interest.

2. Defendant Has Failed to Show that COPA Is the Least Restrictive Alternative for Advancing Congress' Compelling Interest

26. Defendant has failed to successfully defend against the plaintiffs' assertion that filter software and the Government's promotion and support thereof is a less restrictive alternative to COPA. The Supreme Court recognized, upon the evidence before it at the time of the issuance of the preliminary injunction in 1999, that:

Filters are less restrictive than COPA. They impose selective restrictions on speech at the receiving end, not universal restrictions at the source. Under a filtering regime, adults without children may gain access to speech they have a right to see without having to identify themselves or provide their credit card information. Even adults with children may obtain access to the same speech on the same terms simply by turning off the filter on their home computers. Above all, promoting the use of filters does not condemn as criminal any category of speech, and so the potential chilling effect is eliminated, or at least much diminished. All of these things are true, moreover, regardless of how broadly or narrowly the definitions in COPA are construed.

Ashcroft, 542 U.S. at 667. The evidence at trial shows that this is still the case today. It remains true, for example, that unlike COPA there are no fines or prison sentences associated with filters which would chill speech. 47 U.S.C. §231(a). Also unlike COPA, as shown by Findings of Fact 68, 78, and 79, filters are fully customizable and may be set for different ages and for different categorizes of speech or may be disabled altogether for adult use. As a result, filters are less restrictive than COPA.

27. Moreover, defendant contends that: (1) filters currently exist and, thus, cannot be considered a less restrictive alternative to COPA; and that (2) the private use of filters cannot be deemed a less restrictive alternative to COPA because it is not an alternative which the government can implement. These contentions have been squarely rejected by the Supreme Court in ruling upon the efficacy of the 1999 preliminary injunction by this court. The Supreme Court wrote:

Congress undoubtedly may act to encourage the use of filters. We have held that Congress can give strong incentives to schools and libraries to use them. It could also take steps to promote their development by industry, and their use by parents. It is incorrect, for that reason, to say that filters are part of the current regulatory status quo. The need for parental cooperation does not automatically disqualify a proposed less restrictive alternative. In enacting COPA, Congress said its goal was to prevent the "widespread availability of the Internet" from providing "opportunities for minors to access materials through the World Wide Web in a manner that can frustrate parental supervision or control." COPA presumes that parents lack the ability, not the will, to monitor what their children see. By enacting programs to promote use of filtering software, Congress could give parents that ability without subjecting protected speech to severe penalties.

Ashcroft, 542 U.S. at 669-670 (internal citation omitted). I agree with the Supreme Court and conclude today that the mere fact that filters currently exist does not indicate that they cannot be a less restrictive or effective alternative to COPA nor does it make them part of the regulatory status quo. I also agree and conclude that in conjunction with the private use of filters, the government may promote and support their use by, for example, providing further education and training programs to parents and caregivers, giving incentives or mandates to ISP's to provide filters to their subscribers, directing the developers of computer operating systems to provide filters and parental controls as a part of their products (Microsoft's new operating system, Vista, now provides such features, *see* Finding of Fact 91), subsidizing the purchase of filters for those who cannot afford them, and by performing further studies and recommendations regarding filters.

3. Defendant Has Failed to Show that Other Alternatives Are Not at Least as Effective as COPA

28. Defendant has also failed to show that filters are not at least as effective as COPA at protecting minors from harmful material on the Web. The first hurdle in this analysis is that there is no showing of how effective COPA will be. However, the evidence shows that at a minimum, COPA will not reach a substantial amount of foreign source sexually explicit materials on the Web, which filters will reach. Findings of Fact 63, 65, 66.

29. COPA will also not be effective because its affirmative defenses including the age verification schemes are not effective.

30. Moreover, based on the recent sparse enforcement history of the obscenity laws detailed in Findings of Fact 132 and 133 and the concern of the Department of Justice that COPA "could require an undesirable diversion of critical investigative and prosecutorial resources that the Department currently invests in . . . prosecuting . . . large-scale and multi district commercial distributors of obscene materials", Pl. Ex. 55; Finding of Fact 131, it is unlikely that COPA will be widely enforced, thus further limiting its effectiveness.

31. The Supreme Court recognized that, on the record before them at the time, filters were "likely more effective as a means of restricting children's access to materials harmful to them." *Ashcroft,* 542 U.S. at 667. I conclude that the evidence in this case now confirms the Supreme Court's prediction.

32. Although filters are not perfect and are prone to some over and under blocking, the evidence shows that they are at least as effective, and in fact, are more effective than COPA in furthering Congress' stated goal for a variety of reasons. For example, as shown by Findings of Fact 68, 78 through 80, 87 through 91, and 92 through 99, filters block sexually explicit foreign material on the Web, parents can customize filter settings depending on the ages of their children and what type of content they find objectionable, and filters are fairly easy to install and use.

D. Vagueness and Overbreadth

37. Facial challenges to legislation are "employed by the Court sparingly and only as a last resort." *Nat'l Endowment for the Arts v. Finley,* 524 U.S. 569, 580 (1998) (quoting *Broadrick v. Oklahoma,* 413 U.S. 601, 613 (1974)). To prevail on their facial challenge to COPA, the plaintiffs must "demonstrate a substantial risk that application of the provision will lead to suppression of speech." *Id.*

1. COPA Is Vague

38. The vagueness doctrine was created to ensure fair notice and nondiscriminatory application of the laws. A statute or regulation fails for vagueness if men of ordinary intelligence must speculate as to the meaning of what the statute or regulation requires or prohibits.41. Although Findings of Fact 122, 123, 128, and 129 demonstrate that Congress intended COPA to apply solely to commercial pornographers, the phrase "communication for commercial purposes", as it is modified by the phrase "engaged in the business", does not limit COPA's application to commercial pornographers. The lack of clarity in these phrases results in Web sites, which only receive revenue from advertising or which generate profit for their owners only indirectly, from being included in COPA's reach. Since the enforcement of COPA could result in prosecution of the plaintiffs in this case, it is reasonable for the plaintiffs to fear prosecution under COPA. The uncertainty resultant from the vagueness of "communication for commercial purposes" would cause the plaintiffs' speech to be chilled or self censored, as demonstrated by Findings of Fact 50, 54, and 57 through 61.

42. As noted above, COPA defines a minor as "any person under 17 years of age." 47 U.S.C. §231(e)(7). Although the government argues that the term minor should be interpreted to mean an older minor, as the Third Circuit noted, such an interpretation would be "in complete disregard of the text" of COPA. *ACLU,* 322 F.3d at 253. As discussed by the Third Circuit, defining minors as "any person under 17 years of age," creates a serious issue with interpretation of COPA since no one could argue that materials that have "serious literary, artistic, political, or scientific value" for a sixteen-year-old would necessarily have the same value for a three-year old. *Id.,* at 253-54. Likewise, what would be "patently offensive" to an eight-year-old would logically encompass a broader spectrum of what is available on the Web than what would be considered "patently offensive" for a sixteen-year-old. Presumably no material covered by COPA would be "designed to appeal to, or [be] designed to pander to, the prurient interest" of a two or four-year old. *Id.,* at 254. As the Third Circuit noted, "[i]n abiding by this definition, Web publishers who seek to determine whether their Web sites will run afoul of COPA cannot tell which of these 'minors' should be considered in deciding the particular content of their Internet postings." *Id.* Thus, the application of the definition of minors to COPA creates vagueness in the statute.

43. I recognize that state laws prohibiting obscene-as-to-minors material have been upheld by the Supreme Court with no discussion of whether they apply to minors of every age or only to older minors. *See e.g. Ginsberg v. State of N. Y.,* 390 U.S. 629 (1968). In a store, the cashier can easily discern if a patron is 10 or 11 years old instead of a claimed age of 17. The same cashier, however, may have trouble discerning whether a patron is 16 years old or 17 years old without some form of photographic identification. Thus, with laws that are concerned with face-to-face transactions, in reality it is only those borderline cases in which a minor is close to the age of majority that are at issue. As a result, in the pre-Internet age, it was not completely necessary to be more specific in delineating what was obscene as to minors of various age groups. However, on the Internet, everyone is faceless and fairly anonymous and, thus, the context is radically changed. The Internet merchant has no viable method of determining whether an individual is 6, 12, 17 or 51 years old. Consequently, we are presented with this novel problem where a general prohibition on materials obscene as to minors creates a vagueness in the context of Internet transactions that is lacking in other situations.

44. COPA does not define the term "as a whole" and the plain language of the statute does not lend itself to a obvious definition of "as a whole" as it might be applied to the Internet. §The Third Circuit concluded in a dictum that the language of COPA clearly demonstrated that each individual "communication, picture, image, graphic image file, article, recording, writing or other matter of any kind" should be considered without context. *ACLU,* 322 F.3d at 252. But, as Justice Breyer noted in his dissent, "as a whole" has been traditionally interpreted in obscenity cases to require an examination of the challenged material within the context of the book or magazine in which it is contained. *Ashcroft,* 542 U.S. at 681 (citing *Roth v. U.S.,* 354 U.S. 476, 490 (1957)). As Justice Kennedy noted in his concurring opinion, "The notion of judging work as a whole is familiar in other media, but more difficult to define on the World Wide Web. It is unclear whether what is to be judged as a whole is a single image on a Web page, a whole Web page, an entire multipage Web site, or an interlocking set of Web sites." 535 U.S. at 592-93. Thus, with the disparate views noted above, and as discussed below, in the context of the Web, I conclude that the use in COPA of the phrase "as a whole" without any further definition, is vague.

45. There is no question that a printed book or magazine is finite, and, as a result, it is very easy to discern what needs to be examined in order to make an "as a whole" evaluation. The same is not true for a Web page or Web site since Web pages and sites are hyperlinked to other Web pages and sites. As demonstrated by online magazines such as Nerve and Salon, even the Web sites for online magazines, without considering the hyperlinks to off-site materials, have greater

depth and breadth than their counterpart in print. *See* Findings of Fact 3, 21, 26. Instead of having a two-hundred page book or an issue of a magazine to look to for context, COPA invokes some undefined portion of the vast expanse of the Web to provide context for material allegedly violating the statute. As a result, a Web publisher cannot determine what could be considered context by a fact finder, prosecutor, or court, and therein lies the source of the vagueness.

46. The vagueness of COPA, like the vagueness of CDA, is especially concerning since they are both content-based regulations. "An impermissible chill is created when one is deterred from engaging in protected activity by the existence of a governmental regulation or the threat of prosecution thereunder." *Aiello v. City of Wilmington,* 623 F.2d 845, 857 (3d Cir. 1980). The plaintiffs have demonstrated, as recounted in Factual Findings 50, 54, and 57 through 61, that COPA has a chilling effect on free speech. The fact that Web publishers are faced with criminal prosecution for an alleged violation of COPA only serves to exacerbate the chilling effect resultant from the vagueness of the terms employed in COPA. Thus, I conclude that COPA is clearly unconstitutionally vague.

2. COPA Is Overbroad

47. "The overbreadth doctrine prohibits the Government from banning unprotected speech if a substantial amount of protected speech is prohibited or chilled in the process." *Free Speech Coalition,* 535 U.S. at 255. The Supreme Court has noted that, "the possible harm to society in permitting some unprotected speech to go unpunished is outweighed by the possibility that protected speech of others may be muted." *Broadrick,* 413 U.S. at 612.

48. Since the vagueness of "communication for commercial purposes" and "engaged in business" would allow prosecutors to use COPA against not only Web publishers with commercial Web sites who seek profit as their primary objective but also those Web publishers who receive revenue through advertising or indirectly in some other manner, the array of Web sites to which COPA could be applied is quite extensive. Such a widespread application of COPA would prohibit and undoubtably chill a substantial amount of constitutionally protected speech for adults.

49. As discussed above, because a story that might have "serious literary value" for a sixteen-year-old could be considered to appeal to the "prurient interest" of an eight-year-old and be "patently offensive" and without "serious value" to that child, Web publishers do not have fair notice regarding what they can place on the Web that will not be considered harmful to "any person under 17 years of age." As the Third Circuit stated in ruling on the efficacy of the 1999 preliminary injunction by this court, "[b]ecause COPA's definition of 'minor' therefore broadens the reach of 'material that is harmful to minors' under the statute to encompass a vast array of speech that is clearly protected for adults . . . the definition renders COPA significantly overinclusive." *ACLU,* 322 F.3d at 268.

50. The affirmative defenses in COPA do not prevent it from sweeping too broadly since they do not verify age, impose additional burdens, and add to the statute's chilling effect.

51. "When a federal court is dealing with a federal statute challenged as being overly broad, it should, of course, construe the statute to avoid constitutional problems, if the statute is subject to such a limiting construction." *New York v. Ferber,* 458 U.S. 747, 769 n.24 (1982). If the statute is not subject to a limiting construction but can be severed so that a constitutional part remains, the statute should be severed accordingly. *Id.* However, a law should not be rewritten by a court so that it can pass constitutional muster. *Am. Booksellers Ass'n,* 484 U.S. at 397.

52. Nothing in the statute references commercial pornographers, for whom the statute was apparently intended, as demonstrated by Findings of Fact 122, 123, 128, and 129. To read such a

limitation into the statute would result in an impermissible rewriting of the statute and assumption of the role of the legislature by this court. The term "minor" is clearly not subject to a narrowing construction, because, as noted by the Third Circuit, acting as if COPA only applied to older minors would be "in complete disregard of the text" of COPA. *ACLU,* 322 F.3d at 253. There is no portion of the statute that could be severed to satisfy the First Amendment since the terms "commercial purposes" and "minor" cannot be removed and leave a viable statute. Thus, I conclude that COPA is unconstitutional as a result of its overbreadth.

V. CONCLUSIONS

I agree with Congress that its goal of protecting children from sexually explicit materials on the Web deemed harmful to them is especially crucial. This court, along with a broad spectrum of the population across the country yearn for a solution which would protect children from such material with 100 percent effectiveness. . . . Despite my personal regret at having to set aside yet another attempt to protect our children from harmful material, I restate today, as I stated when granting the preliminary injunction in this case, that "I without hesitation acknowledge the duty imposed on the Court [as Justice Kennedy observed] and the greater good such duty serves. Indeed, perhaps we do the minors of this country harm if First Amendment protections, which they will with age inherit fully, are chipped away in the name of their protection." 31 F. Supp.2d at 498.

For the forgoing reasons, I conclude that COPA facially violates the First and Fifth Amendment rights of the plaintiffs because: (1) COPA is not narrowly tailored to the compelling interest of Congress; (2) defendant has failed to meet his burden of showing that COPA is the least restrictive and most effective alternative in achieving the compelling interest; and (3) COPA is impermissibly vague and overbroad. Therefore, I will enter a permanent injunction against the enforcement of COPA.

NOTES AND QUESTIONS

1.   **Surprise?** What, if anything, was a surprise in this opinion, given all that came before it? Does this outcome vindicate the majority in *Ashcroft v. ACLU*? The dissent?

2.   **What Now?** If you were a supporter of COPA, what would you do now? Push for resolution in the Supreme Court? But now there are findings of fact that seem to buttress the majority's position, and all five members of the *Ashcroft* majority remain on the Court. Would you abandon COPA (thus avoiding a final determination by the Supreme Court) and try to craft new legislation? But what, exactly, should that legislation provide?

Chapter 20:   Advanced Services

Insert at p. 1027, after the excerpt from Atkinson and Weiser:

In April of 2007, the FCC released a trio of documents related to broadband deployment and business practices and with particular relevance for network neutrality.   These documents consisted of two notices of inquiry and one notice of proposed rule making. In one of the NOIs, the Inquiry Concerning the Deployment of Advanced Telecommunications Capability to All Americans in a Reasonable and Timely Fashion, and Possible Steps to Accelerate Such Deployment Pursuant to Section 706 of the Telecommunications Act of 1996, FCC 07-21, 2007 WL 1135555 (March 12, 2007), the FCC opened up a variety of important questions about the definition, scope, deployment conditions, and conduct incentives of broadband service provision, as summarized in paragraph 11 of the document:

> At the outset, we solicit information consistent with the framework utilized in past reports: (1) how should we define "advanced telecommunications capability"? (2) is advanced telecommunications capability being deployed to all Americans? (3) is the current level of deployment reasonable and timely? and (4) what actions, if any, can be taken to accelerate deployment? As the Commission did in its last section 706 inquiry, we examine additional questions of potential interest to policymakers. In particular, we seek to develop a better understanding of the economic considerations that support the deployment of advanced telecommunications capability. We hope to analyze available information relating to consumer adoption and usage of services requiring advanced telecommunications capability. In addition, we seek comment on the competitiveness of the broadband market and whether there is evidence of anticompetitive conduct in this market.

The Commission did not propose actions in that item, but posed a broad range of open questions. In the companion NOI released the same day, the Commission delved somewhat more deeply into questions of industry practice and the incentives and ability to engage in anticompetitive conduct. An excerpt is below, followed by separate statements by two commissioners expressing dissatisfaction with what they perceive as the FCC's slow pace toward regulation of such potential conduct.

In the Matter of Broadband Industry Practices, Notice of Inquiry
FCC 07-31, 2007 WL 1135556 (March 22, 2007)

By the Commission: Chairman Martin and Commissioners Tate and McDowell issuing separate statements; and Commissioners Copps and Adelstein concurring and issuing separate statements.

10. In this Notice of Inquiry, we seek to enhance our understanding of the nature of the market for broadband and related services, whether network platform providers and others favor or disfavor particular content, how consumers are affected by these policies, and whether consumer choice of broadband providers is sufficient to ensure that all such policies ultimately benefit consumers. We ask for specific examples of beneficial or harmful behavior, and we ask whether any regulatory intervention is necessary.

11.   Over a year ago, the Commission issued a Policy Statement "offer[ing] guidance and insight into its approach to the Internet and broadband" consistent with Congress's direction in sections 230 and 706.   In that Policy Statement, the Commission announced the following principles:

- *To encourage broadband deployment and preserve and promote the open and interconnected nature of the public Internet*, consumers are entitled to access the lawful Internet content of their choice.

- *To encourage broadband deployment and preserve and promote the open and interconnected nature of the public Internet*, consumers are entitled to run applications and use services of their choice, subject to the needs of law enforcement.

- *To encourage broadband deployment and preserve and promote the open and interconnected nature of the public Internet,* consumers are entitled to connect their choice of legal devices that do not harm the network.

- *To encourage broadband deployment and preserve and promote the open and interconnected nature of the public Internet*, consumers are entitled to competition among network providers, application and service providers, and content providers.

12.   Since that time, the Commission has had the occasion to review several providers' practices.· In several proceedings evaluating wireline mergers, the Commission found that no commenter had alleged that the entities engage in packet discrimination or degradation, and that, given conflicting incentives, it was unlikely that the merged companies would do so. Nonetheless, the Commission specifically recognized the applicants' commitments to act in a manner consistent with the principles set forth in the Policy Statement, and their commitments were incorporated as conditions of their mergers. Likewise, in its review of the Adelphia-Time Warner-Comcast transaction, the Commission found that the transaction was not likely to increase incentives for the applicants to engage in conduct harmful to consumers, and found no evidence that the applicants were operating in a manner inconsistent with the Policy Statement.

13.   The Commission, under Title I of the Communications Act, has the ability to adopt and enforce the net neutrality principles it announced in the Internet Policy Statement. The Supreme Court reaffirmed that the Commission "has jurisdiction to impose additional regulatory obligations under its Title I ancillary jurisdiction to regulate interstate and foreign communications."   Indeed, the Supreme Court specifically recognized the Commission's ancillary jurisdiction to impose regulatory obligations on broadband Internet access providers.[1]

14.   We seek a fuller understanding of the behavior of broadband market participants today, including network platform providers, broadband Internet access service providers, other broadband transmission providers, Internet service providers, Internet backbone providers, content and application service providers, and others. First, we ask commenters to describe today's packet management practices. That is, do providers treat different packets in different ways? How and why? Are these providers operating consistent with the Policy Statement? Are there specific examples of packet management practices that commenters consider reasonable or unreasonable? More specifically, are providers engaging in packet management that is helpful or

---

[1] *Brand X*, 545 U.S. at 996 ("[T]he Commission remains free to impose special regulatory duties on facilities-based ISPs under its Title I ancillary jurisdiction. In fact, it has invited comment on whether it can and should do so.").

harmful to consumers? For example, during times of congestion, do providers prioritize packets for latency-sensitive applications such as voice calls, video conferencing, live video, or gaming? Do providers prioritize packets for safety- and security-related applications such as health monitoring, home monitoring, and emergency calls? Do providers block packets containing child pornography, spyware, viruses, or spam? Do providers offer parental controls that block packets containing sexually explicit material? Do providers manage packets to improve their network performance, engineering, or security? Do providers deprioritize or block packets for certain content when the providers or their affiliates offer similar content, or do providers prioritize packets containing their own content over packets containing similar content from unaffiliated providers? Do providers deprioritize or block packets containing material that is harmful to their commercial interests, or prioritize packets relating to applications or services in which they have a commercial interest? Are any of these packet management practices in place to implement other legal requirements? Are there other packet management practices of which the Commission should be aware? Commenters should provide specific, verifiable examples with supporting documentation, and should limit their comments to those practices that are technically feasible today.

15. Next, we ask commenters to describe today's pricing practices for broadband and related services. Do providers charge different prices for different speeds or capacities? Given the greater availability of bandwidth-intensive applications, do providers charge a premium to download a particular amount of content? Do broadband providers charge upstream providers for priority access to end users? Should our policies distinguish between content providers that charge end users for access to content and those that do not? Do providers currently discriminate in the prices they charge to end users and/or upstream providers? Does behavior vary depending on the number of broadband Internet access service providers offering service in a geographic area? With regard to all practices commenters describe in response to the questions in paragraphs 8 and 9, we ask whether providers disclose their practices to their customers, to other providers, to application developers, and others. Do they offer their subscribers the option to purchase extra bandwidth or specialized processing? How have consumers responded to these pricing practices? How have higher speed broadband networks changed the value proposition for consumers? Are the real prices (*i.e.*, price per Mbps) paid by consumers for broadband nevertheless falling?

7. We next ask whether the Policy Statement should be amended. Do commenters believe that the specific practices described in response to the questions in paragraphs 8 and 9 are helpful or harmful to consumers? In light of the responses to paragraphs 8 and 9, are there specific changes to the Policy Statement that commenters would recommend? We also ask whether we should incorporate a new principle of nondiscrimination. If so, how would "nondiscrimination" be defined, and how would such a principle read? Would it permit any exclusive or preferential arrangements among network platform or access providers and content providers? How would a principle of non-discrimination affect the ability of content and access providers to charge their customers different prices, or to charge them at all?

8. Finally, does the Commission have the legal authority to enforce the Policy Statement in the face of particular market failures or other specific problems? What specific conduct or other factors give rise to any such problems? Does the ever increasing intermodal competition among broadband providers prevent such problems from developing in the first place? If the Commission were to promulgate rules in this area, what would be the challenges in tailoring the rules only to reach any identified market failures or other specific problems, and not to prevent policies that benefit consumers? Would regulations further our mandate to "encourage the deployment on a reasonable and timely basis of advanced telecommunications capability to all

Americans"? Assuming it is not necessary to adopt rules at this time, what market characteristics would justify the adoption of rules?

CONCURRING STATEMENT OF
COMMISSIONER MICHAEL J. COPPS

We live in a world where a very few concentrated broadband providers exercise powerful and not always consumer-friendly control over the pipes that come into our homes and businesses. While we welcome telephone companies and cable providers competing to sell high-speed services, FCC statistics show that together these duopoly operators control some 96 percent of the residential broadband market, with too many consumers lacking a choice even between those two providers. Wireless and broadband over powerline are exciting prospects, but the reality is we are nowhere near seeing the kind of ubiquitous third or fourth player necessary to turn broadband into a vibrantly competitive market.

If eventually we develop a truly competitive marketplace with consumers enjoying broadband speeds like those available to our counterparts in other industrial countries, we can step back and rely on the genius of that marketplace. But in the meantime, the concentrated providers out there increasingly have the ability—and some think the business incentive—to build networks with traffic management policies that could restrict how we use the Internet. I haven't taught history for many years, but I remember enough of it to know that if someone has both the technical capacity and the commercial incentive to control something, it's going to get tried.

Don't take my word for it. It was the *Wall Street Journal* that said large carriers "are starting to make it harder for consumers to use the Internet for phone calls or swapping video files." The more powerful and concentrated our facilities providers grow, the greater their motivation will be to close off Internet lanes and block IP byways. After all, some have already touted their support for segregating Internet traffic by charging premium tolls for passage for favored websites, while consigning everyone else's websites and applications to bumpy travels in steerage.

This brings us to the item before us. It really puts the Commission at a crossroads and the path we choose has the potential to recast and shape the Internet for years to come. At issue is whether a few broadband behemoths will be ceded gatekeeper control over the public's access to the full bounty of the Internet. We have a choice to make.

Down one road lies a FCC committed to honor and preserve the fundamental openness that made the Internet so great—a place of freedom and choice where anyone with a good idea and a little tech-savvy can create an idea or business with global reach. On this road the FCC would adopt policies to ensure that the Internet remains a dynamic technology for creating economic and educational opportunity, a fierce economic engine for innovation and entrepreneurship, and a tool for the sustenance and growth of democracy across the land.

Down the other road lies a FCC that, while it celebrates the Internet, sits idly by as broadband providers amass the power and technical ability to dictate where you can go and what you can do on the Internet. This FCC would see no public interest harms when providers set up gated communities and toll booths on the Internet, altering the openness that has characterized this medium from the very start and endangering the principles of packet equality and non-discrimination. Make no mistake—the practical effect of what is being proposed by some network operators is to invert the democratic genius of the Internet. The original idea was to have neutral dumb networks with intelligence invested at the edges, with you and me and millions of other users. Now some seem bent on making the pipe intelligent and all-controlling even while they make all of us users at the edges dumb. Maybe the Internet entrepreneurs of the future will have to seek permission to innovate from the owner of the broadband pipe. That would be really hard to square with what I think should be our responsibility at the FCC, and that is to do everything we can to preserve the openness that made the Internet so great. You know what? I have enough confidence in this technology and enough confidence in American innovation and creativity to believe we can get to the promised land without that kind of discrimination.

How did we get to this unfortunate junction? Let's review a little history. Back in 2003, in a speech at the New America Foundation, I suggested the Internet as we know it could be dying. Some thought that was a rather controversial claim at the time, I know, but let's look at what has happened since. In 2005, the Commission decided to reclassify broadband transmission facilities as Title I "information services" rather than Title II "telecommunications services." To the uninitiated this sounds like semantics. But it had real consequences. That's because the nondiscrimination obligations that attach to telecommunications traffic and which were vital to keeping the Internet open in the dial-up era no longer apply to broadband services.

So when the Commission set off on this course, I asked my colleagues to at least adopt an Internet Policy Statement. They did, and I appreciate that, and as a result, today the Commission has a public document that summarizes the basic rights of Internet end-users. The Internet policy statement states that consumers are entitled to: access content; run applications and services; connect devices to the network; and enjoy competition among network providers, application and service providers and content providers. So far, so good.

But time has taught us that something is missing from this document and another step is needed. In a world where big and concentrated broadband providers are searching for new business models and suggesting that web sites may have to pay additional tolls for the traffic they generate, we need to keep our policies current. It is time for us to go beyond the original four principles and commit industry and the FCC unequivocally to a specific principle of enforceable non-discrimination, one that allows for reasonable network management but makes clear that broadband network providers will not be allowed to shackle the promise of the Internet in its adolescence.

We should be building on what we have already approved and going with at least a Notice of Proposed Rulemaking with a commitment to move to an Order within a time certain. These are not esoteric, inside-the-Beltway issues—they go to the very core of what kinds of opportunities are going to be available to all of us in this digital age. We're being left behind in broadband globally, the country is paying a steep cost, and we face the stark challenge to decide if we are going to do something about it or not. We're talking here about the greatest small "d" democratic technology platform that has ever existed. Taking another year or two to decide if we want to keep it that way shortchanges the technology, shortchanges consumers and shortchanges our future. I will not dissent from the one small step forward we take today, but I do lament our not making a Neil Armstrong giant leap for mankind.

CONCURRING STATEMENT OF
COMMISSIONER JONATHAN S. ADELSTEIN

Ensuring a Neutral and Open Internet

One hallmark of this Order is that it applies explicit, enforceable provisions to preserve and protect the open and interconnected nature of the Internet, including not only a commitment to abide by the four principles of the FCC Internet Policy Statement but also an historic agreement to ensure that the combined company will maintain a neutral network and neutral routing in its wireline broadband Internet access service. Together, these provisions are critical to preserving the value of the Internet as a tool for economic opportunity, innovation, and so many forms of civic, democratic, and social participation.

Most significantly, the Commission takes a long-awaited and momentous step in this Order by requiring the applicants to maintain neutral network and neutral routing in the provision of their wireline broadband Internet access service. This provision was critical for my support of this merger and will serve as a "5th principle," ensuring that the combined company does not privilege, degrade, or prioritize the traffic of Internet content, applications or service providers, including their own affiliates. Given the increase in concentration presented by this transaction—particularly set against the backdrop of a market in which telephone and cable operators control nearly 98 percent of the market, with many consumers lacking any meaningful choice of providers—it was critical that the Commission add a principle to address incentives for anti-competitive discrimination.

Encouraging Consumer Access to Broadband

Affordable Broadband. We made substantial progress during our review in increasing consumer access to broadband services. These services are increasingly recognized as critical for the growth of small businesses, for persons with disabilities, and as a driver of opportunity in so many aspects our lives, including distance learning and telemedicine. So, the commitment to offer basic broadband service for $10 per month should help lower the cost for many consumers who are just starting to take advantage of the broadband experience. I've said often that we need more bandwidth value in this country, so I am pleased to see this commitment from the applicants. We have heard from many Members of Congress, state and local officials, and community organizations who believe that the ability of the combined company to deliver low priced broadband services was particularly appealing to them.

Broadband Build-Out. I also note that, in response to our call for conditions, AT&T has committed to provide broadband services to 100% of their territory by the end of 2007. A ubiquitous broadband commitment is key because people all over this country want access to the opportunities that flow from this technology, no matter where they live. While I support adopting this commitment as a condition of the merger, it alone will not be a panacea. It would have been substantially improved by the inclusion of more specific, quantifiable, and enforceable commitments for rural and low income consumers, who deserve to enjoy the benefits of this transaction, too.

I am particularly pleased that AT&T also has committed to increase its build-out of wireless broadband services. As a condition of this merger, AT&T will jumpstart service in the under-used 2.3 GHz band by agreeing to a specific construction commitment over the next three and a half years. AT&T already has conducted a number of successful trials on the spectrum and is running a commercial WiMAX network in Pahrump, Nevada. I want to see more deployment in the 2.3 GHz band. In addition to divesting its 2.5 GHz wireless broadband holdings, AT&T has met my challenge by committing today to a specific level of buildout by July 2010. Much like the Sprint-Nextel merger, I am hopeful that this build-out commitment will prove a catalyst to the entire Wireless Communications Service. Like a rising tide that lifts all boats, AT&T's work in this band will be a boon for other wireless broadband providers looking to provide service in the 2.3 GHz band.

  Stand-Alone DSL.   Another major victory for consumers is the ability to purchase broadband services without having to buy a whole bundle of traditional telephone service. So, I fully support the applicants' commitment to provide a meaningful stand-alone DSL option for consumers who want access to broadband services but who want to "cut the cord." Consumer advocates have strongly supported this condition, which should expand the options available for residential and small business consumers who are interested in relying on wireless or Internet phone service for their voice connections.

  We have shown greater attention in this Order to the stand-alone DSL condition because it must be implemented fairly in order to be a meaningful option for consumers. In the previous merger of then SBC with AT&T, we conditioned our support on the offer of a similar naked DSL service. I was disappointed when that offer was made to consumers at a price point that seemed designed to make it unattractive for consumers, virtually at the same level as the entire bundled offering. In California, for example, consumers who were actually able to learn of the availability of stand-alone DSL, which had not been advertised, were quoted a rate of $44.99 per month, a mere one dollar less than the least expensive regular bundle of DSL and phone service. So, it is especially meaningful here that we were able to reach agreement for AT&T to offer the service at $19.95. Particularly in combination with the Internet neutrality conditions adopted today, this stand-alone DSL offering should create an opportunity for the development of competitive Voice over Internet Protocol (VoIP) services. This condition has the potential both to give consumers more options and flexibility in their broadband and voice services, and to spur the development of competition and choice.

The third document the Commission released on April 16, 2007, was a companion NPRM, Development of Nationwide Broadband Data to Evaluate Reasonable and Timely Deployment of Advanced Services to All Americans, Improvement of Wireless Broadband Subscribership Data, and Development of Data on Interconnected Voice over Internet Protocol (VoIP) Subscribership, FCC 07-17, 2007 WL 1135554 (Feb. 26, 2007). In that NPRM the FCC primarily solicits comments and proposes to make rules governing information gathering about the state of broadband services in the United States. As stated in paragraph 1 of the NPRM:

> The Commission has consistently recognized the critical importance of broadband services to the nation's present and future prosperity and is committed to adopting policies to promote the development of broadband services, including broadband Internet access services. In this Notice of Proposed Rulemaking (Notice), we seek comment about how the Commission can continue to acquire the information it needs to develop and maintain appropriate broadband policies. First, we seek comment about how the Commission can best ensure that it receives sufficient information about the availability and deployment of broadband services nationwide, particularly in rural and other hard-to-serve areas, including tribal lands. Second, we seek comment about how the Commission can

improve the data about wireless broadband Internet access services that it currently collects on FCC Form 477. Third, we ask whether we should modify the speed tier information we currently collect. Fourth and finally, we seek comment about how the Commission can best collect information about subscribership to interconnected voice over Internet Protocol (interconnected VoIP) service. Information about broadband availability and deployment throughout the nation is essential to enable us to assess the success of our broadband policies in order to further discharge our statutory mandate, pursuant to section 706 of the Telecommunications Act of 1996, to "encourage the deployment on a reasonable and timely basis of advanced telecommunications capability to all [Americans]."

NOTES AND QUESTIONS

1.   **Carts before Horses, or Open Barn Doors?** The Commission's three broadband documents discussed above mostly raise questions: questions about the need for, and potential impacts of, policies that would induce increased broadband deployment, increased broadband consumption, and reduced potential for anticompetitive conduct by broadband network operators and service providers. The commissioners do not disagree about those questions or their importance. But they do disagree on what to do while the questions are pending. What explains the adamant and dramatic statements by Commissioners Copps and Adelstein in favor of bolder and more sweeping steps toward regulation now? Do those commissioners just wish to put the cart before the horse and regulate even without knowing the answers to the underlying questions, as posed in the NOIs and NPRM? Or, are the other commissioners risking leaving the proverbial barn doors open too long by naively asking questions that, by time they are answered, will be moot because irreparable harm to the broadband market will have occurred? What is balance of risks implicit in each side's approach? Who is right? Can Commissioners Copps and Adelstein reconcile concurring with a document that states no evidence of anticompetitive discrimination had been shown, while at the same time arguing that regulations to govern such conduct are necessary?

2.   **Rhetoric versus Action.** What concrete steps do Commissioners Copps and Adelstein propose for the broadband market? They talk in broad terms about network neutrality and its potential benefits. But what do they mean by network neutrality and what specific rules do they articulate?

3.   **Wireless Network Neutrality?** Even as the debate over network neutrality rages in the wireline world, Professor Tim Wu has proposed extending the idea to the wireless world. In a working paper titled "Wireless Network Neutrality: Cellular *Carterfone* and Consumer Choice in Mobile Broadband," New America Foundation, Wireless Futures Program Working Paper #17 (February 2007), Professor Wu argues that actions taken by the four competing, nationwide wireless carriers block innovation in applications for wireless devices and that such actions should be prohibited by regulation. In an opposing paper, Robert Hahn, Robert Litan, and Hal Singer argue that the issues and market conditions relevant to Wu's paper are distinct from those raised by the wireline network neutrality debate and that those distinctions render his proposals particularly inapt. We note these developments to highlight the expanding nature of the network neutrality debate and possible directions of that debate going forward.

4.   **The FTC Enters the Network Neutrality Fray.** This past April, the Federal Trade Commission held hearings on network neutrality. With Congress and the FCC already being lobbied hard by both sides of the issue, what is to be gained by adding yet another government

entity to the fray? It turns out there may be good reason. As discussed in Chapter 20 at pp. 984-1011, the FCC has declined to impose common-carrier obligations on provision of cable modem or DSL services. Accordingly, in the absence of regulation or action by Congress that changes this exemption or of specific enforcement actions by the FCC, there may be no basis for FCC intervention against refusals by a network to carry particular content. Antitrust law might therefore be called upon by future plaintiffs, and the FTC would likely have to make enforcement decisions related to network neutrality. After analyzing the relevant competition policy issues, an FTC Staff Report on Broadband Connectivity Competition Policy (which was adopted 5-0 by the Commission) concluded that policymakers should be cautious in considering regulations to address network neutrality concerns.   The FTC Staff Report is available at http://www.ftc.gov/reports/broadband/v070000report.pdf.

Voice over IP developments

Insert at p. 1047, just before the section on competition:

The Minnesota Public Utilities Commission v. FCC
483 F.3d 570 (8th Cir. 2007)

Opinion for the court filed by Circuit Judge BYE, in which Circuit Judges HEANEY and COLLOTON concur.
BYE, Circuit Judge:

Before the court are consolidated petitions for review which challenge an order of the Federal Communications Commission (FCC) preempting state regulation of telecommunication services which utilize a relatively new technology called Voice over Internet Protocol (VoIP). The FCC preempted state regulation after determining it would be impractical, if not impossible, to separate the intrastate portions of VoIP service from the interstate portions, and state regulation would conflict with federal rules and policies. We . . . affirm the FCC's order and deny the petitions for review.

I

VoIP is an internet application utilizing "packet-switching" to transmit a voice communication over a broadband internet connection. In that respect, it is different from the "circuit-switching" application used to route traditional landline telephone calls. In circuit-switched communications, an electrical circuit must be kept clear of other signals for the duration of a telephone call. Packet-switched communications travel in small digital packets along with many other packets, allowing for more efficient utilization of circuits. While sophisticated, the application is also more cost effective than traditional circuit switches.

VoIP communications also differ from traditional circuit-switched telephone communications in another significant way. The end-to-end geographic locations of traditional landline-to-landline telephone communications are readily known, so it is easy to determine whether a particular phone call is intrastate or interstate in nature. Conversely, VoIP-to-VoIP communications originate and terminate at IP addresses which exist in cyberspace, but are tied to no identifiable geographic location. For example, a VoIP customer residing in Minnesota but visiting New York could connect a laptop computer to a broadband internet connection and communicate with a next-door neighbor via computer back in Minnesota, while the next day the same "caller" could be in Los Angeles and talk to the same friend who now happens to be in Los Angeles as well. The Internet would recognize both communications as taking place between the same two IP addresses, but when considering the geographic locations of the caller and recipient, the first call would be interstate while the second intrastate in nature.

Similarly, in VoIP-to-landline or landline-to-VoIP communications, known as "interconnected VoIP service," the geographic location of the landline part of the call can be determined, but the geographic location of the VoIP part of the call could be anywhere in the universe the VoIP customer obtains broadband access to the Internet, not necessarily confined to the geographic location associated with the customer's billing address or assigned telephone number. Furthermore, using the North American Numbering Plan (NANP) (i.e., the system of using a three-digit area code followed by a seven-digit number) or a VoIP customer's billing address as "proxies" for the originating or terminating points of interconnected VoIP communications causes some interstate calls to appear to be intrastate in nature and vice versa. In the example used above, if we assume both the caller and recipient had Minnesota billing addresses and NANP numbers with Minnesota area codes, both communications would appear to be intrastate Minnesota calls if the billing addresses or NANP numbers were used as proxies for the originating and terminating points of the communications, even though the first was an interstate call between New York and Minnesota and the second an intrastate California call.

A distinction can be drawn, however, between what is referred to as "nomadic" VoIP service and "fixed" VoIP service. Nomadic service is the type described above, where a VoIP customer can use the service "nomadically" by connecting with a broadband internet connection anywhere in the universe to place a call. Fixed VoIP service describes the use of the same technology, that is, converting a voice communication into digital packets before transmitting it to another location, but in a way where the service is used from a fixed location. For example, cable television companies offer VoIP service to their customers, but when they do so the ensuing transmissions use the cable running to and from the customer's residence. As a result, the geographic originating point of the communications can be determined. Thus, when VoIP is offered as a fixed service rather than a nomadic service, the interstate and intrastate portions of the service can be more easily distinguished.

The use of VoIP technology has grown rapidly, and with this growth has come controversy over the technology's regulatory status. Some VoIP providers contend the service should be classified for regulatory purposes as an "information service" which, like the Internet itself, Congress has deemed should be free from almost all federal and state regulation. Meanwhile, many state regulators argue VoIP service should be classified as a "telecommunications service," with the intrastate aspects of the service regulated at the state level and the interstate aspects regulated at the federal level. A primary point of contention about how VoIP service should be regulated deals with the provision of emergency 911 services, which necessitate the identification of a caller's geographic location.

With this oversimplified summary of VoIP service as a backdrop, we consider the particular dispute which gave rise to the consolidated petitions for review now before our court.

II

On July 15, 2003, the Minnesota Department of Commerce (MDOC) filed a complaint with the Minnesota Public Utilities Commission (MPUC) alleging the DigitalVoice services being offered by Vonage Holdings Corporation (Vonage), which utilized VoIP technology, were "telephone services." The complaint further alleged Vonage was offering such services without complying with the state regulations governing telephone services - such as obtaining a service permit and filing a tariff listing the prices, terms, and conditions applicable to DigitalVoice. As a result of the MDOC's complaint, the MPUC ordered Vonage to comply with the Minnesota regulations applicable to telephone service and to cease and desist offering DigitalVoice services within the state until it did so.

In response to the MPUC's order, Vonage filed a petition with the FCC requesting it to preempt the order on the grounds Vonage was a provider of "information services," rather than a "telecommunications carrier, " and thus exempt from state regulation for its DigitalVoice service. In the alternative, Vonage invoked the "impossibility exception" of 47 U.S.C. §152(b), which allows the FCC to preempt state regulation of a service which would otherwise be subject to dual federal and state regulation where it is impossible or impractical to separate the service's intrastate and interstate components, and the state regulation interferes with valid federal rules or policies. *See La. Pub. Serv. Comm'n v. FCC*, 476 U.S. 355, 368 (1986) (indicating the FCC can preempt state law "where compliance with both federal and state law is in effect physically impossible"); *see also id.* at 375 n.4 ("FCC pre-emption of state regulation [should be] upheld where it [is] not possible to separate the interstate and the intrastate components of the asserted FCC regulation.").

Vonage also filed suit against the MPUC in federal district court seeking to enjoin enforcement of the cease and desist order. The district court granted a permanent injunction which barred the MPUC from enforcing its order, concluding Vonage was providing "information services" rather than "telecommunication services" and therefore not subject to state regulation. *Vonage Holdings Corp. v. Minn. PUC*, 290 F. Supp. 2d 993, 999 (D. Minn. 2003). The MPUC appealed the ruling to the Eighth Circuit.

While the MPUC's appeal was pending, the FCC issued an order addressing Vonage's petition. In its order, the FCC adopted Vonage's alternative position, which is, irrespective of whether Vonage's services should be characterized as "telecommunication services" or "information services," the FCC determined it was appropriate to preempt state regulation because it was impossible or impractical to separate the intrastate components of VoIP service from its interstate components. The FCC stated: "[T]he practical inseverability of other types of IP-enabled services having basic characteristics similar to DigitalVoice *would* likewise preclude state regulation . . .. Accordingly, to the extent other entities, such as cable companies, provide VoIP services, we *would* preempt state regulation to an extent comparable to what we have done in this Order." *In re Vonage Holdings Corp.*, 19 F.C.C.R. 22404, 22424 (2004) (emphasis added).

The four primary issues raised in the consolidated petitions are whether the FCC's order is arbitrary and capricious because it (1) failed to make a threshold determination about whether VoIP services were "information services" or "telecommunications services," (2) determined it is impractical or impossible to separate the intrastate components of VoIP service from its interstate components, (3) determined state regulation of VoIP service conflicts with federal regulatory policies, and (4) preempted emergency 911 telephone service requirements. A fifth issue raised in the petition filed by the Public Service Commission of the State of New York is whether ¶32 of the FCC's order arbitrarily preempted "fixed" VoIP services offered by cable television companies, even though the intrastate components of such service can more easily be separated from the interstate components of such services. [The court held this issue not to be ripe for review]

III

This court reviews a federal agency's decision under the Administrative Procedure Act (APA) and will set aside the decision only when it is "arbitrary, capricious, an abuse of discretion, or otherwise not in accordance with law." *Mages v. Johanns*, 431 F.3d 1132, 1139 (8th Cir. 2005) (quoting 5 U.S.C. §706(2)(A)).

The first issue is whether the FCC arbitrarily or capriciously failed to classify VoIP service as either an "information service" or a "telecommunications service." The FCC concluded state regulation of VoIP service should be preempted regardless of its regulatory classification because it was impossible or impractical to separate the intrastate components of VoIP service from its interstate components. The FCC deferred resolution of the regulatory classification of VoIP service in its order because the issue was already "the subject of [its] *IP-Enabled Services Proceeding* where the Commission is comprehensively examining numerous types of IP-enabled services, including services like DigitalVoice." *In re Vonage Holdings Corp.*, 19 F.C.C.R. at 22411 n.46. As to this order, the FCC contends the dispositive nature of the impossibility exception made it unnecessary to first classify VoIP service.

In *Nat'l Cable & Telecomms. Ass'n v. Gulf Power Co.*, 534 U.S. 327, 338 (2002), the Supreme Court described as "sensible" the FCC's decision not to determine "whether [Internet services] are cable services" under the Communications Act, given the FCC's decision that such a determination was unnecessary for the FCC to assert jurisdiction over pole-attachment rates for Internet traffic. 534 U.S. at 337. This case is similar to Gulf Power. The impossibility exception, if applicable, is dispositive of the issue whether the FCC has authority to preempt state regulation of VoIP services. It was therefore sensible for the FCC to address that question first without having to determine whether VoIP service should be classified as a telecommunication service or an information service.

The next issue is whether the FCC arbitrarily or capriciously concluded the impossibility exception applies to VoIP services. As already discussed, the "impossibility exception" of 47 U.S.C. §152(b) allows the FCC to preempt state regulation of a service if (1) it is not possible to separate the interstate and intrastate aspects of the service, and (2) federal regulation is necessary to further a valid federal regulatory objective, i.e., state regulation would conflict with federal regulatory policies. We address each of the components of the impossibility exception in turn.

The FCC determined on the basis of the record before it that there was no "practical means . . . of directly or indirectly identifying the geographic location of a DigitalVoice subscriber." *In re Vonage Holdings Corp.*, 19 F.C.C.R. at 22418. The FCC further emphasized

> the significant costs and operational complexities associated with modifying or procuring systems to track, record and process geographic location information as a necessary aspect of the service would substantially reduce the benefits of using the Internet to provide the service, and potentially inhibit its deployment and continued availability to consumers. . . .The Internet's inherently global and open architecture obviates the need for any correlation between Vonage's DigitalVoice service and its end users' geographic locations.

Id. at ¶¶23-24. Additionally, the FCC recognized communications over the Internet were very different from traditional landline-to-landline telephone calls because of the multiple service features which might come into play during a VoIP call, i.e., "access[ing] different websites or IP addresses during the same communication and [] perform[ing] different types of communications simultaneously, none of which the provider has a means to separately track or record [by geographic location]." *Id.* at ¶25.

It was proper for the FCC to consider the economic burden of identifying the geographic endpoints of VoIP communications in determining whether it was impractical or impossible to separate the service into its interstate and intrastate components. Service providers are not required to develop a mechanism for distinguishing between interstate and intrastate communications merely to provide state commissions with an intrastate communication they can then regulate. In addition, the issue whether VoIP services can be separated into interstate and intrastate components is a largely fact-driven inquiry requiring a high level of technical expertise. As noted above, in such situations we accord a high level of deference to the informed decision of the agency charged with making those fact findings. After carefully examining the record in this case, as well as the parties' arguments, we conclude the FCC did not arbitrarily or capriciously determine it was impractical or impossible to separate the intrastate components of VoIP service from its interstate components.

Because of the high level of deference we owe to the FCC on this fact-specific issue, it is unnecessary to justify our decision by countering all of the petitioners' challenges to the FCC's fact-findings, and instead we focus our attention on the primary contention raised on appeal—the alleged inconsistency between the FCC order challenged here and a subsequent order issued by the FCC addressing VoIP 911 service. *See* In Re IP-Enabled Servs. & E911 Requirements for IP-Enabled Service Providers (*911 Order*) 20 F.C.C.R. 10245 (2005). The petitioners contend the two orders are inconsistent—while the first finds it impractical or impossible to identify the geographic end-points of VoIP communications, the second requires VoIP providers to do just that for the purpose of ensuring customers using VoIP service can obtain 911 services when the need arises. The petitioners contend the 911 Order requires Vonage to pinpoint the geographic source of the call. They argue it necessarily follows that the intrastate and interstate components of the service can then be separated.

The 911 Order does not provide a basis for concluding the order before us is arbitrary and capricious. Contrary to the assertions of the state public utilities commissions, the 911 Order also recognizes the practical difficulties of accurately determining the geographic location of VoIP customers when they place a phone call. *See 911 Order,* 20 F.C.C.R. 10245 at 10259 ("VoIP service providers often have no reliable way to discern from where their customers are accessing VoIP service."); *see also Nuvio Corp. v. FCC,* 473 F.3d 302, 303, 304 (D.C. Cir. 2007) (denying a petition for review challenging the 911 Order and noting "there are no means yet available to easily determine the location of a caller using interconnected VoIP service [and] it is not yet technologically feasible to detect automatically the location of nomadic VoIP callers."). Recognizing this practical difficulty, the FCC devised a temporary solution requiring VoIP service providers to have their customers register the physical location at which they would first utilize VoIP service, and to also provide a means for customers to update these registered locations. Under this temporary fix, responses to 911 calls would be routed to the registered location, which may not be the same as the actual location where the call was placed. Thus, in both the order before us and the 911 Order, the FCC recognized the practical difficulties of determining the geographic location of nomadic VoIP phone calls.

Similarly, we emphasize the limited scope of our review of the FCC's decision. Our review is limited to the issue whether the FCC's determination was reasonable based on the record existing before it at the time. If, in the future, advances in technology undermine the central rationale of the FCC's decision, its preemptive effect may be reexamined.

The FCC also determined state regulation of VoIP service would interfere with valid federal rules or policies. Because the FCC deferred the regulatory classification of VoIP service to its IP-Enabled Services Proceeding, the FCC examined whether state and federal policies would conflict regardless of whether DigitalVoice were classified as an information service or a telecommunications service. The FCC determined conflicts would exist in either event.

With respect to the conflicts which would exist if DigitalVoice were classified as a telecommunications service, the FCC explained "Vonage would be considered a nondominant, competitive telecommunications provider for which the Commission has eliminated entry and tariff filing requirements." *In re Vonage Holdings Corp.,* 19 F.C.C.R. at 22415. In contrast, Minnesota law would compel a tariffed offering. Similarly, Minnesota law has entry requirements under which Vonage would be required to obtain a certificate of authority from the MPUC before offering its services in Minnesota. The FCC noted it eliminated tariff requirements for the purpose of promoting competition and the public interest, and Minnesota's tariff requirement "*may actually harm consumers* by impeding the development of vigorous competition." *Id. at 22416 ¶20* (emphasis added).

With respect to the conflicts which would develop if DigitalVoice were classified as an information service, the FCC referred to its "long-standing national policy of nonregulation of information services." *Id.* at ¶21. The FCC has promoted a market-oriented policy allowing providers of information services to "burgeon and flourish in an environment of free give-and-take of the market place without the need for and possible burden of rules, regulations and licensing requirements." *Id.* (internal quotations and citations omitted). Thus, any state regulation of an information service conflicts with the federal policy of nonregulation.

The FCC's conclusions regarding the conflicts between state regulation and federal policy deserve "weight" - the agency has a "thorough understanding of its own [regulatory framework] and its objectives and is uniquely qualified to comprehend the likely impact of state requirements." *Geier v. Am. Honda Motor Co.,* 529 U.S. 861, 883 (2000) (internal quotations and citations omitted). Competition and deregulation are valid federal interests the FCC may protect through preemption of state regulation. After carefully considering the positions presented by both sides of this dispute, we conclude the FCC did not arbitrarily or capriciously determine state regulation of VoIP service would interfere with valid federal rules or policies.

The next issue is whether the FCC arbitrarily or capriciously preempted Minnesota's 911 requirements. Minnesota "includes as one of its entry conditions the approval of a 911 service plan 'comparable to the provision of 911 service by the [incumbent] local exchange carrier.'" *In re Vonage Holdings Corp.,* 19 F.C.C.R. at 22430 (quoting Minn. R. §7812.0550, Subpt 1). The FCC determined this requirement "inextricably links pre-approval of a 911 plan to becoming certificated to offer services in the state" and thus "operates as an entry regulation." *Id.* Because the FCC had already determined there was no practical way for Vonage to identify the geographic location of the calls placed by its customers, Vonage could not comply with this entry regulation and thus the requirement effectively barred Vonage from entry into Minnesota. As a consequence, the FCC preempted "this requirement along with all other entry requirements contained in Minnesota's 'telephone company' regulations." *Id.*

Relying upon the obligations imposed upon VoIP providers under FCC's subsequent 911 Order (issued June 3, 2005), the MPUC contends Vonage could have complied with Minnesota's 911 requirement. We disagree. The FCC's VoIP 911 requirements did not exist when the MPUC asserted jurisdiction over Vonage, or when the FCC issued the order at issue here. As a consequence, it is improper for the MPUC to rely upon the 911 Order to challenge the reasonableness of the FCC decision now before us. *See* 47 U.S.C. §405(a) (providing that a party must file a petition for agency reconsideration before it may seek judicial review of an issue over which the FCC has had no "opportunity to pass"). Moreover, there is no guarantee Minnesota would accept as sufficient for its purposes the requirements imposed upon VoIP providers under the 911 Order. As the FCC noted in the 911 Order, there are a variety of "differences in state laws and regulations governing the provision of 911 service." *911 Order,* 20 F.C.C.R. at 10251 n.34. Because of the nomadic nature of VoIP service, we agree with the FCC there is a need for "setting national rules for 911/E911 service[]." *Id.* at 10259. The FCC did not arbitrarily or capriciously preempt Minnesota's 911 requirements.

NOTES AND QUESTIONS

1.   **Fish or Fowl?** As noted above in connection with the Time Warner decision (providing interconnection to VoIP providers through wholesale carriers), the FCC has refused to classify Voice over IP as either an information or telecommunications service. This reluctance to classify

Voice over IP parallels the earlier reluctance to classify broadband as either an information or telecommunications service. In the Vonage case above, however, the FCC did not want to allow the court to make the decision for the agency (as occurred with respect to broadband, where the Ninth Circuit took the first crack at the issue in the Portland v. FCC decision). Consequently, it decided that VoIP was either an "interstate telecommunications service" or an "information service" and that, in either case, state regulation was preempted.

2.   Fixed Line VoIP. The FCC's decision classified both "nomadic VoIP providers"—i.e, ones like Vonage that allow individuals to bring their VoIP phones with them when they travel— but also fixed line VoIP service providers, such as those provided by cable companies (and sometimes called Digital Voice services). The Eighth Circuit, however, declined to rule on the proper classification of fixed line VoIP, concluding that the FCC's decision was pure dicta and that the facts of the case before it did not require it to either uphold or reject that classification. How would you rule on fixed line VoIP? Does the rationale for classifying it as either an interstate telecommunications service or an information service hold up?

3.   Consumer Protection. State utility commissions traditionally have protected consumers from all sorts of telecommunications-related scams. Are they prohibited from exercising any form of oversight over VoIP? How about state attorneys general or state courts authorized to enforce common law fraud claims?

4.   Impediments to Competition. The FCC states that Minnesota's rules would impede entry by VoIP providers. Meanwhile, the FCC is developing its own rules for VoIP providers. As you read the excerpts below, ask yourself how the rules the FCC applies differ in their implications for competition from the rules preempted in the order above.

NUVIO CORPORATION, PETITIONER v. FEDERAL COMMUNICATIONS COMMISSION, ET Al.
473 F.3d 302 (D.C. Cir. 2006)

Opinion for the court filed by Circuit Judge GRIFFITH, in which Chief Judge GINSBURG and Circuit Judge KAVANAUGH concur. Concurring opinion filed by Judge KAVANAUGH.

GRIFFITH, Circuit Judge:

Petitioners, providers of the newly-emerging technology of Internet telephone service, challenge an order of the Federal Communications Commission ("Commission" or "FCC") that gave them only 120 days to do what is already required of providers of traditional telephone service: transmit 911 calls to a local emergency authority. We deny their consolidated petition for review because we conclude that the Commission adequately considered not only the technical and economic feasibility of the deadline, inquiries made necessary by the bar against arbitrary and capricious decision-making, but also the public safety objectives the Commission is required to achieve.

I.

One of the many dramatic changes the Internet has brought to telecommunications has been the development of interconnected Voice over Internet Protocol ("VoIP") service, which allows a caller using a broadband Internet connection to place calls to and receive calls from other callers using either VoIP or traditional telephone service. *E911 Requirements for IP-Enabled Service Providers, First Report and Order and Notice of Proposed Rulemaking,* 20 F.C.C.R. 10245, 10246 n.1 (2005) ("*Order*"). From a caller's perspective, interconnected VoIP service is, for the most part, similar to traditional telephone service, and its users reasonably expect it to function the same. But two additional capabilities of VoIP service undermine those expectations when callers try to use 911 emergency services. VoIP service allows callers to choose what are called "non-native" area codes. For example, a customer living in the District of Columbia can use an area code from anywhere in the country. Some interconnected VoIP providers ("IVPs") also offer "nomadic" service, which allows a VoIP telephone call to be made and received from wherever the user can establish a broadband connection. (By contrast, "fixed" VoIP telephone service can only be used from a dedicated, fixed connection—typically in a home or office.) As attractive as these two features may be, each makes it difficult for IVPs to provide the local callers the 911 emergency service they expect and upon which they rely. Routers designed to direct 911 calls cannot recognize non-native area codes, and unlike traditional and wireless telephone service, there are no means yet available to easily determine the location of a caller using interconnected VoIP service. IVPs, which were not required to do otherwise, failed to use dedicated trunks (communications paths connecting two switching systems, used to establish an end-to-end connection) set aside for routing calls to a local emergency call center (known as a public safety answering point or "PSAP") and instead routed 911 calls to administrative lines that had not been designed and were not staffed to handle emergency calls. *Id.* at 10246 n.2 (documenting various instances in which consumers were unable to contact emergency help after dialing 911 using an interconnected VoIP service). The resulting tragedies gave rise to the *Order* at issue.

The Commission, which had previously been reluctant to regulate this nascent industry for fear of hindering its development, *see, e.g., IP-Enabled Services, Notice of Proposed Rulemaking,* 19 F.C.C.R. 4863, 4864 (2004) ("*Notice of Proposed Rulemaking*" or "*NPRM*") (noting that IP-enabled services had developed "in an environment that is free of many of the regulatory obligations applied to traditional telecommunication services"), decided that an immediate solution was required to "discharge[] the Commission's statutory obligation to promote an effective nationwide 911/E911 emergency access system," *Order,* 20 F.C.C.R. at 10266. The Commission thus ordered that

> within 120 days of the effective date of this Order, an interconnected VoIP provider must transmit all 911 calls, as well as a call back number and the caller's "Registered Location" for each call, to the PSAP, designated statewide default answering point, or appropriate local emergency authority that serves the caller's Registered Location.

Id. ¶37 (citations omitted).

In effect, the *Order* requires that all IVPs, including those that offer nomadic service using non-native area codes, ensure that their users are able to reach local emergency services when making 911 calls. To do so, IVPs must route all 911 calls using the technology known as Automatic Number Identification ("ANI") or pseudo-ANI, if necessary. ANI "identifies the calling party and may be used as a call back number." *47 C.F.R. §20.3.* A pseudo-ANI is "[a] number, consisting of the same number of digits as ANI, that is not a North American Numbering Plan telephone directory number and may be used in place of an ANI to convey special meaning." *Id.* Because local selective routers are not capable of delivering non-native numbers to a local PSAP, pseudo-ANIs are used to temporarily mask the true number with a local number to facilitate processing by the local selective router for delivery to the PSAP. *See id.* The Commission was less stringent in requiring the use of Automatic Location Information (ALI), which provides an emergency dispatcher with the geographic location of the caller, because it is not yet technologically feasible to detect automatically the location of nomadic VoIP callers. The *Order* only requires, therefore, that IVPs ensure that 911 calls are routed to the *registered* and not the *actual* location of each 911 caller. *See Order,* 20 F.C.C.R. at 10271. IVPs, however, must provide a way for consumers to update their registered locations in a timely fashion. *See id.* These interconnected IVP 911 calls must also be routed through the Wireline E911 network. *See id.* at 10269.

The Commission did not dictate a specific manner for IVPs to provide E911 access. Instead, the Commission noted that IVPs could satisfy these requirements by interconnecting directly with the E911 network through incumbent local exchange carriers ("ILECs"), *see id.* at 10268, by interconnecting indirectly through a third party, *see id.* at 10267, or by any other solution that results in E911 access, *see id.* Finally, the *Order* requires that interconnected VoIP providers notify every customer, new and existing, about "the circumstances under which E911 service may not be available through the interconnected VoIP service or may be in some way limited by comparison to traditional E911 service." *Id.* at 10272.

II.

Under the Administrative Procedure Act, which governs our review of this challenge, petitioners' burden is to show that the *Order* is "arbitrary, capricious, an abuse of discretion, or otherwise not in accordance with law," *see* 5 U.S.C. §706(2)(A). They rely upon three arguments to meet that burden. First, petitioners assert that the *Order*'s 120-day deadline for IVPs to provide E911 service to their users of nomadic, non-native VoIP service is an unexplained departure from the Commission's precedent made without adequate regard to economic and technological obstacles. Petitioners also fault the *Order* for requiring that IVPs connect to the Wireline E911 network but failing to impose a corresponding duty on ILECs to permit this connection. Finally, petitioners contend that the Commission did not give adequate notice of the substance of the *Order*. We consider these arguments in turn and find each wanting.

A. *The FCC decision to require all IVPs—including providers of nomadic, non-native VoIP service—to provide E911 access within 120 days.*

Petitioners assert that the Commission disregarded record evidence that the 120-day deadline was not feasible because there was no demonstrated way to overcome the technical and practical obstacles to implement E911 for providers of nomadic, non-native VoIP service. But this argument fails in the face of substantial contrary record evidence that the nation's largest interconnected VoIP provider had already procured a technical solution to meet the deadline. The Commission noted that Intrado, a third-party competitive local exchange carrier, was already prepared to offer a technological solution that met the *Order*'s requirements, even for providers of nomadic, non-native service. *Order,* 20 F.C.C.R. at 10267. At the time the *Order* was promulgated and in advance of the 120-day deadline, Intrado was already offering a service that "enables the delivery of a VoIP subscribers [sic] address and call back number to the most geographically relevant [PSAP] . . ., thereby accommodating the nomadic capability inherent in their VoIP service." Ex Parte Letter from M. Boyd, Intrado, to M.H. Dortch, FCC, WC Docket No. 04-36 (Apr. 25, 2005). Vonage, the nation's largest VoIP provider, agreed with Verizon, the ILEC controlling the Wireline E911 network in its territory, that it would use Intrado's service "to deliver both caller's location and call back number to emergency services personnel for 911 calls placed throughout Verizon's [28-state] territory," and would do so by November 4, before the November 28, 2005 deadline. Ex Parte Letter from W.B. Wilhelm, Vonage, to K.J. Martin, FCC, WC Docket No. 04-36 (May 9, 2005).

The Commission also relied on IVP trials that demonstrated E911 access was possible for providers of nomadic, non-native VoIP service. For example, Qwest and Vonage conducted a test of VoIP E911 access in King County, Washington. This test included both an experimental means of PSTN access and a messaging component used to deliver the calling party's location automatically. Petitioners' focus on the failed experimental access component ignores the successful messaging component of the trial that demonstrated VoIP E911 access was in fact possible. In recounting the results of this trial, Qwest noted that, rather than using this failed experimental access, an IVP could provide E911 service using a combination of Qwest's tarriffed access to the Wireline E911 network and third party support services. Vonage had also successfully tested E911 access for nomadic VoIP in Newport, Rhode Island. Petitioners seize upon two elements of this Newport test to argue that it is an unreliable basis for the *Order*. First, there is only one PSAP in small Rhode Island and so this test could not address the critical issue of routing calls to the wrong PSAP. Second, the state and not an ILEC owns the selective router and so there is no issue of providing access to the E911 Wireline network. Petitioners have no doubt identified elements in this test that provide some grounds to distinguish them from what the *Order* demands, but the general success of the Rhode Island test, combined with the substantial deference we owe the FCC's predictive judgments, overcomes the petitioners' objections. *See, e.g., ILGWU v. Donovan,* 722 F.2d 795, 821 (D.C. Cir. 1983) ("Predictive judgments about areas that are within the agency's field of discretion and expertise" are entitled to "particularly deferential" treatment).

We must also address the petitioners' claim that the Commission erred by failing to distinguish between the technological obstacles faced by nomadic or non-native VoIP providers and those faced by fixed, native providers. They allege the Commission based the *Order* on the technological capabilities associated with fixed VoIP service and overlooked the unique challenges posed by nomadic, non-native VoIP service. But the Commission in fact considered the unique technological challenges of nomadic VoIP, *see Order,* 20 F.C.C.R. at 10259 (noting that "certain [nomadic or portable] VoIP services pose significant E911 implementation challenges"), and taking stock of those challenges, did not require that IVPs determine the *actual* location of nomadic VoIP users because it "is not always technologically feasible for providers of interconnected VoIP service to automatically determine the location of their end users without end users' active cooperation," *id.* at 10271. Instead, the Commission determined that IVPs must provide only the *registered* location of the nomadic VoIP user making a 911 call, *see id.,* and called for comment on the feasibility of automatically determining the geographic location of nomadic VoIP users, *see id.* at 10276-77.

Petitioners' argument that the Commission overlooked the economic cost of implementing the *Order*'s 120-day deadline highlights that our task under the arbitrary or capricious standard is to determine only whether an agency's decision "'was based on a consideration of the relevant factors and whether there has been a clear error of judgment,'" *Motor Vehicle Mfrs. Ass'n of U.S., Inc. v. State Farm Mut. Auto. Ins. Co.,* 463 U.S. 29, 43 (1983). Petitioners overlook a countervailing interest that the Commission must consider and we must respect-the threat to public safety. When, as is the case with the FCC, Congress has given an agency the responsibility to regulate a market such as the telecommunications industry that it has repeatedly deemed important to protecting public safety, the agency's judgments about the economic cost of its regulations must take into account its duty to protect the public. The Commission is required to consider public safety by both its enabling act, see Communications Act of 1934 §1, 47 U.S.C. §151 ("so as to make available, so far as possible . . . [a] world-wide wire and radio communication service with adequate facilities at reasonable charges . . . *for the purpose of promoting safety of life and property through the use of wire and radio communications*") (emphasis added), and the Wireless Communication and Public Safety Act of 1999 §3, 47 U.S.C. §615 ("shall encourage and support efforts by States to deploy comprehensive end-to-end emergency communications infrastructure and programs, based on coordinated statewide plans, including seamless, ubiquitous, reliable wireless telecommunications networks and enhanced wireless 9-1-1 service"). The Commission here weighed public safety against the economic cost of compliance with the *Order* and found that, "[w]hile 120 days is an aggressively short amount of time in which to comply with these requirements, *the threat to public safety if we delay further is too great* and demands near immediate action." *Order,* 20 F.C.C.R. at 10266-67 (emphasis added).

Because the Commission has reasonably determined that nomadic, non-native VoIP E911 access is technologically feasible, any argument about the time period required for implementation is nothing more than a quarrel over relative costs and benefits. In this case, the Commission has weighed the cost of an "aggressive" implementation scheme—a 120-day deadline—against the cost in human lives, and found in favor of public safety. *See id.* at 10266 ("We find that this requirement most appropriately discharges the Commission's statutory obligation to promote an effective nationwide 911/E911 emergency access system by recognizing the needs of the public safety community to get call back and location information and balancing those needs against existing technological limitations of interconnected VoIP providers."); *cf. Public Citizen v. Auchter,* 702 F.2d 1150, 1157 (D.C. Cir. 1983) ("Delays that might be altogether reasonable in the sphere of economic regulations are less tolerable when human lives are at stake."). We may not disturb its determination where, as here, the Commission has considered relevant factors and has articulated a reasoned basis for its conclusion. *See State Farm,* 463 U.S. at 42-43. When viewed in this light, we cannot agree that the 120-day deadline is arbitrary or capricious.

Petitioners' final challenge to the 120-day deadline is that it represents an unexplained departure from long-standing precedent. The precedent, so the argument goes, was established when the FCC gave more time for wireless and satellite phones and other new technologies to implement 911 capabilities than the aggressive deadline it has imposed on the new VoIP telephone service market. Petitioners are right that an agency departing from precedent "must provide a principled explanation for its change of direction." *Nat'l Black Media Coalition v. FCC,* 775 F.2d 342, 355 (D.C. Cir. 1985). But surely different technologies may reasonably bear different regulatory burdens. It is not apparent to us that the regulation of satellite or wireless phones is clear precedent for the regulation of information technology service providers. No doubt each involves telephone communications, but the differences between satellite and wireless phone service on the one hand and VoIP service on the other are such that the Commission has previously refused to classify IP-enabled services as telecommunications carriers. We give deference to agency expertise used to distinguish its prior cases from present controversies. Even if the Commission's regulatory approach to these other telecommunications services provided a precedent for VoIP service, the Commission provided a reasoned explanation for adopting a different approach by expressly noting that "the record indicates that the network components that have been developed to make wireless E911 possible can also be used for VoIP E911, which should make the implementation process simpler and far less expensive than the initial upgrades necessary for wireless E911." *Order,* 20 F.C.C.R. at 10274

Because petitioners acknowledge that some type of E911 regulation is necessary, *see* Petitioners' Br. at 19, this petition for review is, in essence, a challenge only to where the FCC has drawn the regulatory "line," and we have previously and repeatedly given the Commission "wide discretion to determine where to draw administrative lines." *AT&T Corp. v. FCC,* 220 F.3d 607, 627 (D.C. Cir. 2000). Based on the record evidence, the demonstrated safety concerns, and our deference to the Commission's predictive judgments, we conclude that the *Order*'s 120-day deadline was neither arbitrary nor capricious.

B. *The FCC requirement for IVP connectivity to the Wireline E911 network without a corresponding obligation on ILECs.*

The *Order* requires IVPs to utilize the Wireline E911 network generally owned by the ILECs, but it failed to impose a duty on ILECs to provide that access. Petitioners argue that this different treatment of the ILECS was error. We find no error for the simple reason that the record contained evidence that major ILECs were cooperating with nomadic IVPs and "increasingly offering E911 solutions that allow VoIP providers to interconnect directly to the Wireline E911 network through tariff, contract, or a combination thereof." *Order,* 20 F.C.C.R. at 10268. There is record evidence, for example, that Qwest, Bellsouth, and Verizon were cooperating with IVPs to provide access to the Wireline E911 network. Although there is some evidence to suggest that a few ILECs were not always cooperative, *see* Petitioners' Reply Br. at 10 n.15, there was ample evidence of significant and increasing ILEC cooperation with IVPs and, in the Commission's view, that cooperation removed any need to impose a duty upon ILECs to permit connectivity. That is a judgment we wisely leave alone as "predictions regarding the actions of regulated entities are precisely the type of policy judgments that courts routinely and quite correctly leave to administrative agencies," *Public Utils. Comm'n of State of Cal. v. FERC,* 24 F.3d 275, 281 (D.C. Cir. 1994).

For the foregoing reasons, the petition for review is denied.

[Concurring opinion of Judge Kavanaugh is omitted.]

NOTES AND QUESTIONS

1.   **What Alternatives?** In acknowledging that some E911 mandate was warranted, what do the petitioners want instead of the FCC's policy? Would their alternatives serve the public as well? Consider how the FCC could have been stricter in its regulation. Did it strike a good balance between avoiding competitive impediments and protecting the public?

2.   **Wireless versus VoIP E911.** Over the last decade, wireless providers have been afforded considerable leeway as they developed technologies to enable consumers to access 911 from their phones and for "automatic location information" (ALI) to be delivered to the public safety answer points (PSAPs). In the order upheld above, VoIP providers were mandated to adopt such technologies within 120 days. Why the difference in treatment? Do you agree with the FCC's rationale?

3.   **Caveat Emptor.** Should the FCC be in the business of requiring all telephone services to provide emergency contacts? If, for example, consumers use VoIP services in a complementary way to conventional or wireless telephone services that already provide 911 service, then to what extent is the FCC benefiting consumers? Why not let VoIP providers differentiate themselves, with some offering E911 in an effort to displace other forms of telephony and some not providing it but offering a lower cost in an effort to become a more complementary service? In such cases, a requirement of disclosure about the existence of 911 connectivity might suffice. Is the FCC effectively prejudging the role that VoIP will eventually play in the marketplace?

4.   **PSAPs and ALI.** The FCC exercises jurisdiction over the carriers, not over the PSAPs. In many cases, PSAPs have limited funding sources and thus have not upgraded from their antiquated systems, meaning that, in some cases, they are not able to process the ALI even when delivered to them. Should carriers be required to adopt the capability of delivering such information even if it will not be useful to individual PSAPs?

5.   **Public Choice Theory in Action?** One popular theory of regulation is that the regulatory process is used by particular firms to gain an advantage over their competitors. This theory, which is often termed "public choice theory" or "rent seeking explanations," could be used to suggest that the E911 mandate foisted upon VoIP providers reflected an effort by incumbent phone companies to make life more difficult for their competitors. Is that a fair characterization?

**VONAGE HOLDINGS CORPORATION, PETITIONER v.
FEDERAL COMMUNICATIONS COMMISSION, ET AL.**
2007 WL 1574611 (D.C. Cir., June 1, 2007)

Opinion for the court filed by Circuit Judge TATEL, in which Circuit Judges EDWARDS and GARLAND concur.

TATEL, Circuit Judge:

Petitioners, providers of voice over internet protocol services (VoIP), challenge a Federal Communications Commission order requiring them to contribute to the Universal Service Fund (USF). Specifically, they claim that, in requiring such contributions, the Commission exceeded its authority under the Telecommunications Act of 1996 and acted arbitrarily and capriciously by (1) analogizing VoIP to wireline toll service for the purposes of setting the presumptive percentage of VoIP revenues generated interstate or internationally, (2) requiring pre-approval for traffic studies submitted by VoIP providers but not for those submitted by wireless providers, and (3) suspending the "carrier's carrier rule" with respect to VoIP. We conclude that the Commission has statutory authority to require VoIP providers to make USF contributions and that it acted reasonably in analogizing VoIP to wireline toll service for purposes of setting the presumptive percentage of VoIP revenues generated interstate and internationally. [While upholding the core of the FCC's ruling, the court vacated the Commission's pre-approval of traffic studies and suspension of the carrier's carrier rule as to VoIP providers.]

I.

In March 2004, the Federal Communications Commission issued a notice of proposed rulemaking calling for comments on how best to regulate a range of internet protocol-enabled services, including voice over internet protocol, an internet-based service offering "multidirectional voice functionality, including, but not limited to, services that mimic traditional telephony." *In re IP-Enabled Services*, 19 F.C.C.R. 4863, 4866 n.7 (2004). Perhaps most significantly for VoIP's future, the Commission asked whether it should classify VoIP as a "telecommunications service" or an "information service." If classified as a telecommunications service, VoIP would be subject to mandatory Title II common carrier regulations, 47 U.S.C. §153(44), but as an information service it would not. *See Nat'l Cable & Telecomms. Ass'n v. Brand X Internet Servs.*, 545 U.S. 967, 975-77 (2005). The Commission also requested comment on a range of narrower questions, including—most relevant to this case—whether VoIP providers should be required to contribute to the Universal Service Fund (USF).

The USF is a funding stream the Commission uses to subsidize telecommunications and information services in rural and high-cost areas, as well as for schools, libraries, and low-income households. §The USF receives its funding from businesses in the telecommunications sector; some businesses are required by statute to contribute while others must contribute only when the Commission has, in its discretion, required them to do so. Specifically, the Act mandates contributions from "[e]very telecommunications carrier that provides interstate telecommunications services." 47 U.S.C. §254(d). Moreover, under its permissive contribution authority, the Commission may demand USF contributions from "[a]ny other provider of interstate telecommunications . . . if the public interest so requires." *Id.*

Two years later and following public comment, the Commission issued an order requiring providers of "interconnected" VoIP services to contribute to the USF. *In re Universal Service Contribution Methodology,* 21 F.C.C.R. 7518 (2006) (hereinafter "Order"). Interconnected VoIP services "(1) enable real-time, two-way voice communications; (2) require a broadband connection from the user's location; (3) require IP-compatible customer premises equipment; and

(4) permit users to receive calls from and terminate calls to the PSTN [public switched telephone network]." *Id.* at 7526§.

Deferring a decision on whether to classify VoIP as a telecommunications service or an information service, the Commission grounded its order in its permissive contribution authority and, alternatively, its Title I ancillary jurisdiction. *See Am. Library Ass'n v. FCC*, 406 F.3d 689, 692-93 (D.C. Cir. 2005) (holding that the Commission may regulate under its ancillary jurisdiction when "the subject of the regulation [is both] . . . covered by the Commission's general grant of jurisdiction under Title I of the Communications Act . . . . [and] 'reasonably ancillary to the effective performance of the Commission's various responsibilities.'" (citation omitted)). The Commission gave three reasons for taking this discretionary step. First, USF contributions have declined in recent years, while interconnected VoIP services have "experienced dramatic growth." *Order* at 7528. Thus, requiring contributions from interconnected VoIP providers would "preserve and advance universal service." *Id.* at 7527. Second, interconnected VoIP providers ought to contribute to the USF because "much of the appeal of their services to consumers derives from the ability to place calls to and receive calls from the PSTN, which is supported by universal service mechanisms." *Id.* at 7540. Third, competitive neutrality—a principle that requires advantaging no one technology over another—favors making VoIP providers contribute because they increasingly compete with analog voice service providers, who contribute to the USF. *Id.* at 7541.

Having decided to require VoIP providers to contribute, the Commission turned to the issue of how to calculate the level of such contributions. The Commission assesses USF contributions only on revenues generated from interstate or international calls. For companies connecting landline customers, determining the percentage of interstate or international calls is relatively simple. But for wireless and VoIP providers—whose customers may use their services from many locations and often have area codes that do not correspond to their true location—determining the percentage of interstate and international traffic is more difficult. Given those difficulties, the Commission established—as it has since 1998 for wireless—a "safe harbor" that approximates the percentage of VoIP revenues generated from interstate and international calls. The safe harbor ensures that VoIP providers will not have to make USF contributions on more than a certain percentage of their revenues. As its name suggests, the safe harbor is only a ceiling: VoIP providers may reduce their USF contributions if, through traffic studies, they can show that their actual percentage of interstate and international revenues falls below the safe harbor percentage.

To set the safe harbor level, the Commission sought to identify the "appropriate analogue" for VoIP service. *Order* at 7545. The Commission considered two possibilities: wireline toll service (colloquially referred to as landline long distance), which the Commission presumes to be 64.9% interstate and international, and wireless service, presumed to be 37.1% interstate and international. The Commission selected wireline toll service as the better analogue, giving two reasons for its decision. First, it cited two industry reports, one estimating that 83.8% of VoIP traffic is interstate or international and a second putting the figure at 66.2%—both figures higher than the safe harbor level for wireline toll service. Second, the Commission cited advertisements demonstrating that VoIP providers frequently market their service as a substitute for wireline toll service, noting that many customers purchase such plans in order to "place a high volume of interstate and international calls" and consequently "benefit from the pricing plans the providers offer for such services." *Id.* at 7546.

II.

Section 254(d) of Title 47 states that:

> Every telecommunications carrier that provides interstate telecommunications services shall contribute, on an equitable and nondiscriminatory basis, to the specific, predictable, and sufficient mechanisms established by the Commission to preserve and advance universal service. . . . Any other provider of interstate telecommunications may be required to contribute to the preservation and advancement of universal service if the public interest so requires.

47 U.S.C. §254(d). According to the Commission, section 254(d)'s "permissive portion" (the final sentence) authorizes it to require VoIP providers to contribute to the USF, regardless of whether VoIP is ultimately classified as a "telecommunications service" or an "information service. " Understanding this position requires a brief detour through the regulatory classification decision the Commission has yet to make and the statutory text and case law governing it.

The Act defines both "telecommunications service" and "information service" as "offerings." See 47 U.S.C. §153(46) (defining "[t]elecommunications service" as "the offering of telecommunications for a fee directly to the public"); *id.* §153(20) (defining "[i]nformation service" as "the offering of a capability for generating, acquiring, storing, transforming, processing, retrieving, utilizing, or making available information via telecommunications"). In an order issued several years ago, the Commission advanced a narrow definition of the verb "offer," explaining that cable modem service, even though it contains telecommunications as a component, is not a "telecommunications service" because an "offering" of telecommunications can only be something perceived as telecommunications by the end user viewing the integrated, finished product. *In re Inquiry Concerning High-Speed Access to the Internet Over Cable and Other Facilities,* 17 F.C.C.R. 4798, 4822-23 (2002) (hereinafter "Cable Modem Order"). Because cable modem customers use the service "to access the World Wide Web . . . rather than 'transparently' to transmit and receive ordinary-language messages without computer processing" the Commission concluded that "cable modem service is not a 'stand-alone,' transparent offering of telecommunications." *Brand X,* 545 U.S. at 988 (citing *Cable Modem Order* at 4823-4825). In *Brand X,* the Supreme Court upheld the Commission's interpretation of the word "offer" as reasonable, explaining:

> It is common usage to describe what a company "offers" to a consumer as what the consumer perceives to be the integrated finished product, even to the exclusion of discrete components that compose the product . . . . One might well say that a car dealership "offers" cars, but does not "offer" the integrated major inputs that make purchasing the car valuable, such as the engine or the chassis. It would, in fact, be odd to describe a car dealership as "offering" consumers the car's components in addition to the car itself.

Brand X, 545 U.S. at 990.

Were the Commission to conclude that VoIP is an "offering of telecommunications" and therefore to classify it as a telecommunications service, VoIP providers would fall under section 254(d)'s mandatory contribution language (the first sentence). The scope of the Commission's *permissive* contribution authority, however, does not depend on whether VoIP is considered an "offering" of either telecommunications or information. Rather, the Commission's permissive contribution authority extends to "*provider[s]* of interstate telecommunications." 47 U.S.C. §254(d) (emphasis added). The verb "provide," the Commission explained, "is a different and more inclusive term than 'offer.'" *Order* at 7538-39. Black's Law Dictionary, upon which the Commission relied, defines "'provide'" as "'[t]o make, procure or furnish for future use, prepare. To supply; to afford; to contribute.'" *Id.* (alteration in original) (quoting BLACK'S LAW DICTIONARY 1244 (6th ed. 1990)). Under this definition, the Commission explained, the verb "provide" is broad enough to include the act of supplying a good or service as a component of a larger, integrated product. For instance, under the Commission's interpretation, McDonald's provides beef, as well as hamburgers, and *The Washington Post* provides ink, as well as newspapers.

After concluding that a "provider of telecommunications" need only supply telecommunications as a component of its finished product, the Commission explained that VoIP does in fact include telecommunications as a component. The Act defines "[t]elecommunications" as "the transmission, between or among points specified by the user, of information of the user's choosing, without change in the form or content of the information as sent and received." 47 U.S.C. §153(43). The Commission explained that interconnected VoIP services provide such transmission by virtue of their interconnection with the PSTN:

> [B]y definition, interconnected VoIP services are those permitting users to receive calls from and terminate calls to the PSTN. . . . [W]e find interconnected VoIP providers to be "providing" telecommunications regardless of whether they own or operate their own transmission facilities or they obtain transmission from third parties. In contrast to services that merely use the PSTN to supply a finished product to end users, interconnected VoIP supplies PSTN transmission *itself* to end users.

Order at 7539-40 (footnotes and internal quotation marks omitted.

With this background in mind, we turn to the issues before us.

III.

Where, as here, Congress has delegated interpretive authority to an agency, we review the agency's interpretation of a statute under the familiar two-part test set forth in *Chevron U.S.A. Inc. v. Natural Resources Defense Council, Inc.,* 467 U.S. 837 (1984). We first inquire whether "Congress has directly spoken to the precise question at issue. . . . [and if] the intent of Congress is clear, that is the end of the matter." *Id.* at 842-43. But if "the statute is silent or ambiguous with respect to the specific issue, the question . . . is whether the agency's answer is based on a permissible construction of the statute." *Id.* at 843. In this case, the Commission does not contend that the statute unambiguously places VoIP providers within the phrase "providers of telecommunications." Nor has petitioner CCIA given us any reason to conclude that either the phrase "providers of telecommunications" or the Act's definition of telecommunications unambiguously exempts VoIP providers from the Commission's permissive contribution authority. Thus, we proceed to *Chevron* step two, where "we need not determine that the [agency's] reading . . . is the best possible reading, only that it was reasonable." *AFGE, AFL-CIO, Local 446 v. Nicholson,* 475 F.3d 341, 355 (D.C. Cir. 2007).

The Commission's application of section 254(d) to interconnected VoIP providers involved two discrete decisions: (1) that, unlike the verb "offer," the verb "provide" may apply to the act of supplying a component of an integrated product, and (2) that VoIP providers supply telecommunications as a component of their service.

Provide v. Offer

Recall that in *Brand X* the Supreme Court upheld the narrow definition of "offer" advanced by the Commission. Thus, we now face only two issues: has the Commission reasonably interpreted the word "provide," and was it reasonable for the Commission to give the word "provide" a different meaning than the word "offer"?

As to the first issue, we have little trouble concluding that the word "provide" is sufficiently broad to encompass the Commission's interpretation. Returning to *Brand X*'s car dealership hypothetical, we see nothing strange about the statement that a dealership provides both cars *and* engines. Indeed, one could reasonably interpret the statement that a dealership "does not provide engines" to mean that it sells cars without engines, not that it won't sell disconnected engines.

We also see nothing that would prevent the Commission from interpreting the word "offer" from the demand side (i.e., the consumer's perception of what she receives) and the word "provide" from the supply side (the seller's perception of what she supplies). True, the words have mutual synonyms and can be used interchangeably in some contexts. *See, e.g.,* WEBSTER'S THIRD NEW INTERNATIONAL DICTIONARY 1566, 1827 (1993) (listing "supply" in the definitions of both words). Such similarities, however, provide an insufficient basis for concluding that Congress unambiguously intended the two words to have the same meaning—something it could have accomplished quite simply by using the same word. Indeed, we have repeatedly held that "'[w]here different terms are used in a single piece of legislation, the court must presume that Congress intended the terms to have different meanings.'" *Transbrasil S.A. Linhas Aereas v. Dep't of Transp.*, 791 F.2d 202, 205 (D.C. Cir. 1986) (alteration in original) (quoting *Wilson v. Turnage,* 750 F.2d 1086, 1091 (D.C. Cir. 1984)). Thus, the Commission's construction of the verb "provide" in the phrase "providers of telecommunications" is reasonable under *Chevron* step two.

Telecommunications as a Component of VoIP

CCIA presents three challenges to the Commission's finding that VoIP providers supply telecommunications as a component of their service insofar as they "suppl[y] PSTN transmission *itself* to end users." *Order* at 7540. All three are unpersuasive.

First, CCIA argues that "[a]s only telecommunications, and not 'information services,' may be subject to the USF contribution obligations under the Act, the *VoIP Order* exceeds the scope of the Commission's authority." CCIA Br. 22-23. Spoiling for tomorrow's battle, CCIA insists that "VoIP is an information service, whether or not it is 'interconnected' with the PSTN." CCIA Br. 23-24. But, although "information service" and "telecommunications service" are mutually exclusive categories, CCIA points to no authority supporting its argument that a provider of "information services" cannot also be a "provider of telecommunications" for the purposes of *section 254(d).* Indeed, the Act clearly contemplates that "telecommunications" may be a component of an "information service," defining the latter as "the offering of a capability for generating, acquiring, storing, transforming, processing, retrieving, utilizing, or making available information via telecommunications." 47 U.S.C. §153(20).

Second, CCIA argues that "[u]nder *Brand X,* the Commission is not permitted to isolate the 'transmission element' of VoIP and consider that component in isolation for purposes of Title II classification." CCIA Br. 29. But in *Brand X* the Court merely held that the meaning of the word "offering" in the statute's definition of "telecommunications service" was ambiguous and that the Commission's narrow interpretation was reasonable. The Court had no occasion to consider the meaning of the phrase "providers of telecommunications," much less to determine that the phrase unambiguously demands the same construction the Commission applies to an "offering of telecommunications."

Finally, CCIA argues that "since *interconnected* VoIP always involves change in the 'form or content' of information, it cannot by definition be 'telecommunications.'" CCIA Reply Br. 6. But we have found no indication that anyone made this argument before the Commission, which may explain why the Commission never addressed it. Asked about this at oral argument, CCIA's counsel pointed to two portions of the record where he assured us we would find the argument.

See Oral Arg. Tr. 8 (citing CCIA Reply Br. 5 n.5). Like much of CCIA's brief, however, the cited comments argue only that VoIP is an information service, not that interconnected VoIP providers provide no "telecommunications" as a component of their service. Accordingly, we may not address this argument here.

Finding that the Commission has *section 254(d)* authority to require interconnected VoIP providers to make USF contributions, we have no need to decide whether the Commission could have also done so under its Title I ancillary jurisdiction.

IV.

Next we turn to Vonage's challenges to the safe harbor level, the pre-approval requirement for VoIP traffic studies, and the suspension of the carrier's carrier rule. We review these decisions under the arbitrary and capricious standard, affirming if the Commission "considered the relevant factors and articulate[d] a rational connection between the facts found and the choice made." *Bellsouth Telcoms., Inc. v. FCC,* 469 F.3d 1052, 1056 (D.C. Cir. 2006) (alteration in original) (citation and internal quotation marks omitted). Mindful of Congress's insistence that USF contributions be made "on an equitable and nondiscriminatory basis," we devote particular attention to the Commission's reasons for treating VoIP differently from other technologies. 47 U.S.C. §254(d); see also 47 U.S.C. §254(b)(4) ("All providers of telecommunications services should make an equitable and nondiscriminatory contribution to the preservation and advancement of universal service.").

Safe Harbor Level

The Commission set the safe harbor level by analogizing VoIP to wireline toll service. Because VoIP's functionality and customer profile differ from those of other technologies, reasoning by analogy in this way invites some inevitable imprecision. Vonage, however, does not challenge this aspect of the Commission's method, nor do we think it could, given our cases demanding far less than perfect precision in agency line drawing. In *WJG Telephone Co. v. FCC,* we wrote:

> It is true that an agency may not pluck a number out of thin air when it promulgates rules in which percentage terms play a critical role. When a line has to be drawn, however, the Commission is authorized to make a "rational legislative-type judgment." If the figure selected by the agency reflects its informed discretion, and is neither patently unreasonable nor "a dictate of unbridled whim," then the agency's decision adequately satisfies the standard of review.

675 F.2d 386, 388-89 (D.C. Cir. 1982) (citations omitted).

Vonage argues that the Commission acted arbitrarily and capriciously in choosing wireline toll service instead of wireless service as the analogue for VoIP. The Commission analogized VoIP to wireline toll service principally because VoIP providers market their service as a substitute for wireline toll service and offer pricing plans—typically flat fees for unlimited local and long distance calls—that make the service attractive to customers who place high volumes of interstate and international calls. Questioning this analogy, Vonage argues that, unlike wireline toll service, VoIP functions as an "all-distance service" that enables local as well as long distance and international calls. Vonage also points out that the Commission recognized VoIP's all-distance functionality in two previous decisions, one requiring VoIP providers to ensure 911 service, *In re IP-Enabled Services, E911 Requirements for IP-Enabled Service Providers,* 20 F.C.C.R. 10245, 10246 (2005), and the other requiring them to provide intercept capability for law enforcement, *In re Communications Assistance for Law Enforcement Act and Broadband Access and Services*, 20 F.C.C.R. 14989, 15009-10 (2005).

We agree with Vonage that this difference in capabilities renders the VoIP/wireline toll service analogy imperfect. Perfection, however, is not what the law requires. To prevail, Vonage must show that wireless is so much the better analogue for VoIP that the Commission acted arbitrarily and capriciously by failing to select it. This Vonage has not done. The mere fact that both VoIP and wireless are "all-distance" services hardly compels the conclusion that usage patterns for VoIP are closer to those for wireless than to those for wireline toll service. Vonage's "all-distance" argument also does nothing to disturb the Commission's conclusion that VoIP and wireless are likely to attract different types of customers—with VoIP customers predisposed, on average, to making more long distance and international calls. Indeed, Vonage concedes that VoIP is unlikely to attract customers who make relatively few long distance calls, but nowhere argues that the same is true for wireless. That omission is significant: if VoIP only attracts customers who make high volumes of long distance and international calls but wireless attracts all kinds of customers—perhaps because its mobility appeals even to people who make few long distance calls—then VoIP will carry a greater proportion of long distance and international calls than wireless.

Because Vonage has neither shown why usage patterns for VoIP are more like those for wireless than for wireline toll service nor unsettled the Commission's reasoning regarding the type of customer attracted to VoIP, we have little trouble rejecting its challenge to the safe harbor level. Our confidence in this conclusion is unshaken by Vonage's criticism of the two industry reports cited in the Order. One of those reports estimates that 83.8% of VoIP traffic is long distance or international and the other puts the figure at 66.2%. Vonage insists that these reports, both of whose estimates exceed the 64.9% level selected by the Commission, shed no light on the issue because they estimate world-wide rather than just U.S. VoIP traffic and because nothing suggests that the reports cover only *interconnected* VoIP. For these reasons, we agree with Vonage that the two reports, by themselves, would provide weak support for the Commission's decision. But the Commission did not hang its hat solely on these reports. Indeed, had the Commission done so, we expect that, given the reports' estimates, it would have chosen an even higher safe harbor level. The Commission, moreover, did not overstate the reports' precision, citing them only for the general proposition that "VoIP traffic is predominantly long distance or international." *Order at 7545 ¶53.* Finally, because neither Vonage nor any other commenter submitted studies of its own, the two industry reports appear to be the only record evidence estimating actual VoIP traffic. Given this, we are reluctant to fault the Commission for considering the only available data, however imperfect.

NOTES AND QUESTIONS

1.   **Provide v. Offer.** The *Brand X* case upheld an FCC conclusion that "offering" a service to the public did not include a service embedded within another service (and the opinion featured an analysis of whether pizza delivery included an offer of pizza or merely the pizza bundled with its delivery). By contrast, the case above upheld a conclusion that "providing" a service (here, VoIP) could involve the provision of the embedded service. On this rationale, the FCC held that even if VoIP was an information service, it still relied on and provided consumers with "telecommunications" and thus could be assessed universal service payments. Are these twin conclusions justifiable? Why or why not?

2.   **Non-regulation of VoIP.** At one point, the FCC pronounced its reluctance to regulate VoIP, going so far as to prevent state regulation in the Vonage case discussed above. The last two cases involve the imposition of E911 mandates and universal service responsibilities on VoIP

providers. Is there a new era of VoIP regulation? What other types of regulations might be imposed on VoIP providers? Why the change in rhetoric from the FCC?

3.   VoIP v. Wireless. Note that the FCC imposed a greater responsibility on VoIP providers for paying universal service payments than imposed on wireless providers (i.e., wireless providers have a lower safe harbor for percent of interstate revenue). Does this distinction make sense to you? Should VoIP providers insist on traffic studies to develop particularized findings as to what percentage of their traffic is interstate? Why or why not?

4.   Not All VoIP Services Are Created Equal. Some non-interconnected VoIP services like Skype are still free from regulation. Is that sustainable?

Chapter 21:   Antitrust and Merger Review

Recent merger developments include the U.S. District Court for the District of Columbia's approval, after a lengthy and unusually intensive Tunney Act review of both the Verizon-MCI and SBC-AT&T mergers. The review, which lasted well over a year and which suggests at least some district courts will not be deferential in their Tunney Act reviews of merger settlements, concluded in late March, 2007.   The other major developments were the announcement of the merger between satellite radio carriers XM and Sirius (see note, below), and the FCC's approval (after DOJ approval had already been granted) of the AT&T-Bellsouth merger. An excerpt of the press release announcing the latter decision, and the conditions for approval, follows.

FCC APPROVES MERGER OF AT&T INC. AND BELLSOUTH CORPORATION
2006 WL 3847995 (Dec. 29, 2006)

FCC Press Release:

Washington, D.C. - The Federal Communications Commission today approved the merger of AT&T Inc. (AT&T) and BellSouth Corp. (BellSouth).

The Commission concluded that significant public interest benefits are likely to result from this transaction. Benefits to consumers include:

• Deployment of broadband throughout the entire AT&T-BellSouth in-region territory in 2007.

• Increased competition in the market for advanced pay television services due to AT&T's ability to deploy Internet Protocol-based video services more quickly than BellSouth could do so absent the merger.

• Improved wireless products, services and reliability due to the efficiencies gained by unified management of Cingular Wireless, which is now a joint venture operated by BellSouth and AT&T.

• Enhanced national security, disaster recovery and government services through the creation of a unified, end-to-end IP-based network capable of providing efficient and secure government communications.

• Better disaster response and preparation from the companies because of unified operations.

The Commission's analysis of competitive effects focused on six key groups of services. They are:

• *Special access competition.* The record indicates that, in a small number of buildings in the BellSouth in-region territory where AT&T and BellSouth are the only carriers with direct connections, and where entry is unlikely, the merger is likely to have an anticompetitive effect. The Commission found that a commitment by AT&T to divest indefeasible rights of use (IRUs) to those facilities adequately remedied the competitive harm. The Commission further found that the merger was not likely to result in anticompetitive effects with respect to other special access services that combine one carrier's own facilities with those of another.

• *Retail enterprise competition.* The Commission found that the merger is not likely to have anticompetitive effects for enterprise customers, even though the Applicants currently compete against each other with respect to certain types of enterprise services and some classes of enterprise customers. The Commission found that competition for medium and large enterprise customers should remain strong after the merger because medium and large enterprise customers are sophisticated, high-volume purchasers of communications services and because there will remain a significant number of carriers competing in the market.

• *Mass market voice competition.* The Commission concluded that the merger is not likely to have anticompetitive effects in the mass market. The Commission found that neither BellSouth nor AT&T is a significant present or potential participant in this market outside of their respective regions. Consequently, the Commission found that neither party was exerting significant competitive pressure on the other in their respective in-region territories. The Commission further noted that the rapid growth of intermodal competitors particularly cable telephony providers (whether circuit-switched or Voice over IP (VoIP)) is an increasingly significant competitive force in this market, and anticipates that such competitors likely will play an increasingly important role with respect to future mass market voice competition.

• *Mass market Internet competition.* The Commission found that the merger is not likely to result in anticompetitive effects for mass market high-speed Internet access services. Specifically, the Commission concluded that the merger caused no horizontal effects for these services because neither BellSouth nor AT&T provides any significant level of Internet access service outside of its respective region. The Commission also concluded that, while the merger may result in some vertical integration, the record did not support commenters' conclusions that the merged entity will have the incentive to act anticompetitively in the mass market high-speed Internet access services market.

• *Internet backbone competition.* The Commission concluded that the merger is not likely to result in anticompetitive effects in the Internet backbone market. The Commission found that the merger is not likely to cause the Tier 1 backbone market to tip to monopoly or duopoly, nor is it likely to increase the Applicants' incentive and/or ability to raise rivals' costs.

• *International competition.* The Commission found that the merger is not likely to result in anticompetitive effects for international services provided to mass market, enterprise, or global telecommunications services customers. The Commission also concluded that the merger is not likely to result in anticompetitive effects in the international transport, facilities-based IMTS, or international private line markets.

• In addition, on December 28, 2006, AT&T made a series of voluntary commitments that are enforceable by the Commission and attached as an Appendix. These conditions are voluntary, enforceable commitments by AT&T but are not general statements of Commission policy and do not alter Commission precedent or bind future Commission policy or rules.

Merger Commitments

For the avoidance of doubt, unless otherwise expressly stated to the contrary, all conditions and commitments proposed in this letter are enforceable by the FCC and would apply in the AT&TBellSouth in-region territory, as defined herein, for a period of forty-two months from the Merger Closing Date and would automatically sunset thereafter.

Repatriation of Jobs to the U.S.

AT&T/BellSouth n1 is committed to providing high quality employment opportunities in the U.S. In order to further this commitment, AT&TBellSouth will repatriate 3,000 jobs that are currently outsourced by BellSouth outside of the U.S. This repatriation will be completed by December 31, 2008. At least 200 of the repatriated jobs will be physically located within the New Orleans, Louisiana MSA.

Promoting Accessibility of Broadband Service

1. By December 31, 2007, AT&T/BellSouth will offer broadband Internet access service (*i.e.,* Internet access service at speeds in excess of 200 kbps in at least one direction) to 100 percent of the residential living units in the AT&TBellSouth in-region territory. To meet this commitment, AT&T/BellSouth will offer broadband Internet access services to t least 85 percent of such living units using wireline technologies (the "Wireline Buildout Area"). AT&T/BellSouth will make available broadband Internet access service to the remaining living units using alternative technologies and operating arrangements, including but not limited to satellite and Wi-Max fixed wireless technologies. AT&TBellSouth further commits that at least 30 percent of the incremental deployment after the Merger Closing Date necessary to achieve the Wireline Buildout Area commitment will be to rural areas or low income living units.

2. AT&T/BellSouth will, provide an ADSL modem without charge (except for shipping and handling) to residential subscribers within the Wireline Buildout Area who, between July 1,' 2007, and June 30, 2008, replace their AT&T/BellSouth dial-up Internet access service with AT&T/BellSouth's ADSL service and elect a term plan for their ADSL service of twelve months or greater.

3. Within six months of the Merger Closing Date, and continuing for at least 30 months from the inception of the offer, AT&T/BellSouth will offer to retail consumers in the Wireline Buildout Area, who have not previously subscribed to AT&T's or BellSouth's ADSL service, a broadband Internet access service at a speed of up to 768 Kbps at a monthly rate (exclusive of any applicable taxes and regulatory fees) of $ 10 per month.

Statement of Video Roll-Out Intentions

AT&T is committed to providing, and has expended substantial resources to provide, a broad array of advanced video programming services in the AT&T in-region territory. These advanced video services include Uverse, on an integrated IP platform, and HomeZone, which integrates advanced broadband and satellite services. Subject to obtaining all necessary authorizations to do so, AT&T/BellSouth intends to bring such services to the BellSouth in-region territory in a manner reasonably consistent with AT&T's roll-out of such services within the AT&T in-region territory. In order to facilitate the provision of such advanced video services in the BellSouth in-region territory, AT&T/BellSouth will continue to deploy fiber-based facilities and intends to have the capability to reach at least 1.5 million homes' in the BellSouth in-region territory by the end of 2007. AT&T/BellSouth agrees to provide a written report to the Commission by December 31, 2007, describing progress made in obtaining necessary authorizations to roll-out, and the actual roll-out of, such advanced video services in the BellSouth in-region territory.

Public Safety, Disaster Recovery

1. By June 1, 2007, AT&T will complete the steps necessary to allow it to make its disaster recovery capabilities available to facilitate restoration of service in BellSouth's in-region territory in the event of an extended service outage caused by a hurricane or other disaster.

2. In order to further promote public safety, within thirty days of the Merger Closing Date, AT&T/BellSouth will donate $ 1 million to a section 501(c)(3) foundation or public entities for the purpose of promoting public safety.

Service to Customers with Disabilities

AT&T/BellSouth has a long and distinguished history of serving customers with disabilities. AT&T/BellSouth commits to provide the Commission, within 12 months of the Merger Closing Date, a report describing its efforts to provide high quality service to customers with disabilities.

UNEs

1. The AT&T and BellSouth ILECs shall continue to offer and shall not seek any increase in state-approved rates for UNEs or collocation that are in effect as of the Merger Closing Date. For purposes of this commitment, an increase includes an increased existing surcharge or a new surcharge unless such new or increased surcharge is authorized by the applicable interconnection agreement or tariff, and by the relevant state commission. This commitment shall not limit the ability of the AT&T and BellSouth ILECs and any other telecommunications carrier to agree voluntarily to any different UNE or collocation rates.

Reducing Transaction Costs Associated with Interconnection Agreements

1. The AT&T/BellSouth ILECs-shall make available to any requesting telecommunications carrier any entire effective interconnection agreement, whether negotiated or arbitrated, that an AT&T/BellSouth ILEC entered into in any state in the AT&T/BellSouth 22-state ILEC operating territory, subject to state-specific pricing and performance plans and technical feasibility, and provided, further, that an AT&T/BellSouth ILEC shall not be obligated to provide pursuant to this commitment any interconnection arrangement or UNE unless it is feasible to provide, given the technical, network, and OSS attributes and limitations in, and is consistent with the laws and regulatory requirements of, the state for which the request is made.

3. The AT&T/BellSouth ILECs shall allow a requesting telecommunications carrier to use its pre-existing interconnection agreement as the starting point for negotiating a new agreement.

4. The AT&T/BellSouth ILECs shall permit a requesting telecommunications carrier to extend its current interconnection agreement, regardless of whether its initial term has expired, for a period of up to three years, subject to amendment to reflect prior and future changes of law. During this period, the interconnection agreement may be terminated only via the carrier's request unless terminated pursuant to the agreement's "default" provisions.

Special Access

Each of the following special access commitments shall remain in effect until 48 months from the Merger Closing Date.

1. AT&T/BellSouth affiliates that meet the definition of a Bell operating company in section 3(4)(A) of the Act ("AT&T/BellSouth BOCs") n4 will implement, in the AT&T and BellSouth Service Areas, n5 the Service Quality Measurement Plan for Interstate Special Access Services ("the Plan"), similar to that set forth in the SBC/AT&T Merger Conditions, as described herein and in Attachment A. The AT&T/BellSouth BOCs shall provide the Commission with performance measurement results on a quarterly basis, which shall consist of data collected according to the performance measurements listed therein. Such reports shall be provided in an Excel spreadsheet format and shall be designed to demonstrate the AT&T/BellSouth BOCs' monthly performance in delivering interstate special access services within each of the states in the AT&T and BellSouth Service Areas. These data shall be reported on an aggregated basis for interstate special access services delivered to (i) AT&T and BellSouth section 272(a) affiliates, (ii) their BOC and other affiliates, and (iii) non-affiliates. The AT&T/BellSouth BOCs shall provide performance measurement results (broken down on a monthly basis) for each quarter to the Commission by the 45th day after the end of the quarter. The AT&T/BellSouth BOCs shall implement the Plan for the first full quarter following the Merger Closing Date. This commitment shall terminate on the earlier of (i) 48 months and 45 days after the beginning of the first full quarter following the Merger Closing Date (that is, when AT&T/BellSouth files its 16th quarterly report); or (ii) the effective date of a Commission order adopting performance measurement requirements for interstate special access services.

4. To ensure that AT&T/BellSouth may not provide special access offerings to its affiliates that are not available to other special access customers, before AT&TBellSouth provides a new or modified contract tariffed service under section 69.727(a) of the Commission's rules to its own section 272(a) affiliate(s), it will certify to the Commission that it provides service pursuant to that contract tariff to an unaffiliated customer other than Verizon Communications Inc., or its wireline affiliates. AT&TBellSouth also will not unreasonably discriminate in favor of its affiliates in establishing the terms and conditions for grooming special access facilities.

5. No AT&T/BellSouth ILEC may increase the rates in its interstate tariffs, including contract tariffs, for special access services that it provides in the AT&TBellSouth in-region territory, as set forth in tariffs on file at the Commission on the Merger Closing Date, and as set forth in tariffs amended subsequently in order to comply with the provisions of these commitments.

Transit Service

The AT&T and BellSouth ILECs will not increase the rates paid by existing customers for their existing tandem transit service arrangements that the AT&T and BellSouth ILECs provide in the AT&T/BellSouth in-region territory.

ADSL Service

1. Within twelve months of the Merger Closing Date, AT&T/BellSouth will deploy and offer within the BellSouth in-region territory ADSL service to ADSL-capable customers without requiring such customers to also purchase circuit switched voice grade telephone service. AT&T/BellSouth will continue to offer this service in each state for thirty months after the "Implementation Date" in that state. For purposes of this commitment, the "Implementation

Date" for a state shall be the date on which AT&T/BellSouth can offer this service to eighty percent of the ADSL-capable premises in BellSouth's in-region territory in that state. n13 Within twenty days after meeting the Implementation Date in a state, AT&T/BellSouth will file a letter with the Commission certifying to that effect. In all events, this commitment will terminate no later than forty-two months after the Merger Closing Date.

ADSL Transmission Service

AT&T/BellSouth will offer to Internet service providers, for their provision of broadband Internet access service to ADSL-capable retail customer premises, ADSL transmission service in the combined AT&T/BellSouth territory that is functionally the same as the service AT&T offered within the AT&T in-region territory as of the Merger Closing Date. Such wholesale offering will be at a price not greater than the retail price in a state for ADSL service that is separately purchased by customers who also subscribe to AT&T/BellSouth local telephone service.

Net Neutrality

1. Effective on the Merger Closing Date, and continuing for 30 months thereafter, AT&T/BellSouth will conduct business in a manner that comports with the principles set forth in the Commission's Policy Statement, issued September 23, 2005 (FCC 05-151).

2. AT&T/BellSouth also commits that it will maintain a neutral network and neutral routing in its wireline broadband Internet access service. This commitment shall be satisfied by AT&T/BellSouth's agreement not to provide or to sell to Internet content, application, or service providers, including those affiliated with AT&T/BellSouth, any service that privileges, degrades or prioritizes any packet transmitted over AT&T/BellSouth's wireline broadband Internet access service based on its source, ownership or destination.

This commitment shall sunset on the earlier of (1) two years from the Merger Closing Date, or (2) the effective date of any legislation enacted by Congress subsequent to the Merger Closing Date that substantially addresses "network neutrality" obligations of broadband Internet access providers, including, but not limited to, any legislation that substantially addresses the privileging, degradation, or prioritization of broadband Internet access traffic.

Internet Backbone

1. For a period of three years after the Merger Closing Date, AT&T/BellSouth will maintain at least as many discrete settlement-free peering arrangements for Internet backbone services with domestic operating entities within the United States as they did on the Merger Closing Date, provided that the number of settlement-free peering arrangements that AT&T/BellSouth is required to maintain hereunder shall be adjusted downward to account for any mergers, acquisitions, or bankruptcies by existing peering entities or the voluntary election by a peering entity to discontinue its peering, arrangement. If on the Merger Closing Date, AT&T and BellSouth both maintain a settlement free peering arrangement for Internet backbone services with the same entity (or an affiliate thereof), the separate arrangements shall count as one settlement-free peering arrangement for purposes of determining the number of discrete peering entities with whom AT&T/BellSouth must peer pursuant to this commitment. AT&T/BellSouth may waive terms of its published peering policy to the extent necessary to maintain the number of peering arrangements required by this commitment.. Notwithstanding the above, if within three years after the Merger Closing Date, one of the ten largest entities with which AT&T/BellSouth engages in settlement free peering for Internet backbone services (as measured by traffic volume

delivered to AT&T/BellSouth's backbone network facilities by such entity) terminates its peering arrangement with AT&T/BellSouth for any reason (including bankruptcy, acquisition, or merger), AT&T/BellSouth will replace that peering arrangement with another settlement free peering arrangement and shall not adjust its total number of settlement free peers downward as a result.

2. Within thirty days after the Merger Closing Date, and continuing for three years thereafter, AT&T/BellSouth will post its peering policy on a publicly accessible website. During this three-year period, AT&T/BellSouth will post any revisions to its peering policy on a timely basis as they occur.

Forbearance

1. AT&T/BellSouth will not seek or give effect to a ruling, including through a forbearance petition under section 10 of the Communications Act (the "Act"), 47 U.S.C. 160, or any other petition, altering the status of any facility being currently offered as a loop or transport UNE under section 251(c)(3) of the Act.

2. AT&T/BellSouth will not seek or give effect to any future grant of forbearance that diminishes or supersedes the merged entity's obligations or responsibilities under these merger commitments during the period in which those obligations are in effect.

Wireless

1. AT&T/BellSouth shall assign and/or transfer to an unaffiliated third party all of the 2.5 GHz spectrum (broadband radio service (BRS)/educational broadband service (EBS)) currently licensed to or leased by BellSouth within one year of the Merger Closing Date.

2. By July 21, 2010, AT&T/BellSouth agrees to: (1) offer service in the 2.3 GHz band to 25% of the population in the service area of AT&T|BellSouth's wireless communications services (WCS) licenses, for mobile or fixed point-to-multi-point services, or (2) construct at least five permanent links per, one million people in the service area of AT&T/BellSouth's WCS licenses, for fixed point-to-point services. In the event AT&T/BellSouth fails to meet either of these service requirements, AT&T/BellSouth will forfeit the unconstructed portion of the individual WCS licenses for which it did not meet either of these service requirements as of July 21, 2010; provided, however, that in the event the Commission extends the July 21, 2010, buildout date for 2.3 GHz service for the WCS industry at large ("Extended Date"), the July 21, 2010 buildout date specified herein shall be modified to conform to the Extended Date. The wireless commitments set forth above do not apply to any 2.3 GHz wireless spectrum held by AT&T/BellSouth in the state of Alaska.

NOTES AND QUESTIONS

1.   Competitive concerns. The excerpt above lists some competitive concerns. Do the merger conditions that are discussed later in the excerpt address those concerns?

2.   Basis for Other Conditions? Read the FCC's list of conclusions carefully. How do they relate to the merger conditions? For example, the FCC concludes there is no reason to fear anticompetitive incentives in the Internet market. What relationship, then, do the network neutrality conditions discussed above have to the merger?

3.   More Mergers under Review: XM-Sirius. Satellite radio carriers XM and Sirius announced their intention to merge on March 20, 2007. The merger has sparked substantial debate and controversy, and could be one of the most important telecommunications merger cases in the coming year.